BLESSED
ARE THE PACIFISTS

BLESSED
ARE THE PACIFISTS

The Beatitudes and Just War Theory

Thomas Trzyna

Foreword by Richard A. Kauffman

Herald Press

Scottdale, Pennsylvania
Waterloo, Ontario

Library of Congress Cataloging-in-Publication Data

Trzyna, Thomas N., 1946-
Blessed are the Pacifists : the Beatitudes and just war theory / Thomas
Trzyna.
p. cm.
ISBN 0-8361-9346-6 (pbk. : alk. paper)
1. Sermon on the mount. 2. Pacifism—Religious aspects—Christianity.
3. Peace—Religious aspects—Christianity. 4. Just war doctrine. I. Title.
BT380.3.T79 2006
241'.6242—dc22
2006016223

BLESSED ARE THE PACIFISTS
Copyright © 2006 by Herald Press, Scottdale, Pa. 15683
Published simultaneously in Canada by Herald Press,
Waterloo, Ont. N2L 6H7. All rights reserved
Library of Congress Catalog Card Number: 2006016223
International Standard Book Number: 0-8361-9346-6
Printed in the United States of America
Cover and book design by Alison King

12 11 10 09 08 07 06   10 9 8 7 6 5 4 3 2 1

To order or request information, please call
1-800-759-4447 (individuals); 1-800-245-7894 (trade).
Web site: www.heraldpress.com

To Martha, Alex, and Margaret

Contents

Foreword

I don't know Thomas Trzyna. Never met him. Never talked with him by phone. Never exchanged an email or letter with him. Frankly, I don't owe him anything other than respect. But after reading this splendid little book, I wanted to know something about him. How could an English professor—of all disciplines—teaching at an evangelically oriented university—of all institutions—write a provocative and original apology for the Christian pacifist tradition? His name isn't Yoder! Not even close!

So I set to find out something about this man, and this is what the publisher told me: Thomas Trzyna is an Eagle Scout, a conscientious objector, and a member of the Cal Berkeley class of 1968. He contemplated conflict firsthand while working in an Oakland hospital that treated wounded police officers and Black Panthers, among other victims of urban violence. He is currently working to establish a new university in Vietnam to build sustainable peace and economic progress through education.

Trzyna teaches literature, ethnic studies, world religions, and a course on science and philosophy at Seattle Pacific University. His academic interests have included the study of forgiveness and the sociology of the ethnic studies classroom. He also guides groups of students through the process of writing autobiographies as they define their spiritual lives and find vocations.

Born in Evanston, Illinois, Tom lives in Seattle with his family. He belongs to St. Stephen's Episcopal Church, where he teaches adult education. His wife and two grown children, respectively, work at the University of Washington Department of Psychiatry, Microsoft, and the Fred Hutchinson Cancer Research Center.

An interesting pedigree that may illuminate some things, but it still doesn't explain how this book came to be. And I still don't know the man.

What I do know is that the Christian Church has been of two minds about war and peace. The earliest Christian position, the pacifist one, holds that disciples of Jesus Christ must eschew all uses of violence in order to overcome violence. The dominant position of the Christian church, the just war one, argues that under certain conditions war is regrettably necessary in order to protect the weak and the innocent and to provide national defense. Pacifism on the one hand, justifiable use of force on the other. It's a church-dividing issue with even more serious consequences than our differences over baptism or the Lord's Supper.

Most times when I read advocates of either of the classic Christian perspectives on war and peace I have a sense of having been down this path before. The arguments are well-worn and quite familiar. There is often a sense of moral superiority on either side; both claim an intellectual victory by pointing out the weaknesses of the other.

I had a very different experience reading *Blessed Are the Pacifists*. While Trzyna is in conversation with both traditions, his arguments in favor of the pacifist perspective have a welcome freshness to them. Perhaps it is because he isn't a theologian or an ethicist or because, not having come from a pacifist tradition, he really has no vantage point that he is compelled to defend. But quite frankly, his observations about the thorny problem of human conflict and violence represent the creative and seasoned reflection of a very wise person who does not draw back from responding to the usual just war critiques of pacifism. Trzyna confidently makes a case for peaceful solutions to the problem of war, but he exudes a sense of humility, the kind of humility called for in the Beatitudes, which Trzyna views as the pacifist manual.

I still don't know Trzyna the man, but I've read his book and I commend it to you. It just could start much needed and fruitful conversations between the two Christian camps on war and peace. Like Trzyna says, peacemaking must begin by tending our own gardens. With pacifists on one side and just war advocates on the other side, Christians could do no better than by tending to this ugly divide between us.

Richard A. Kauffman
Senior Editor
The Christian Century

Preface

You can usually get on terms with people
by helping them to kill something.

—Wilfred Thesiger, *The Marsh Arabs*

For without a cement of blood
(it must be human, it must be innocent)
no secular wall will safely stand.

—W. H. Auden, "Horae Canonicae"

Pacifism deserves to be taken seriously as a method for addressing the world's problems. It is not an extremist position, but rather the most moderate and reasonable approach for resolving conflict that has been formulated. The introduction and seven chapters of this short book are an argument in favor of adopting a pacifist approach to conflict resolution. The book does not offer a history of pacifist thought, though it makes references to many well-known thinkers who have written about pacifism and nonviolence, and to many others who have used nonviolent techniques successfully to improve our world.

The Beatitudes in the Sermon on the Mount are the heart of this essay. They present in a compressed form a philosophy of life that is consistent only with a pacifist position. As the heart of Jesus' teaching, they come to us in an order that suggests a comprehensive, step-by-step argument for a way of life that can create peace. The Beatitudes are interpreted here as practical wisdom that must be applied now. Our experience of the world demonstrates to us that, in fact, pacifism is a highly successful philosophy. While the press and history books focus on wars and glorify the pursuit of violence, much of world history is a tale of peaceful negotiation, peaceful coexistence, and charity. Activist and peace studies scholar Elise Boulding has termed this the "hidden side of history." One burden of this book therefore is to serve as a reminder that it is war and violence that are the aberrations, not peace. Still, we stand in danger of becoming more bellicose because our cultures teach us to live double lives. We are to be peaceful at home and in our work but are expected to be ready to put on a mask of patriotism and to kill without mercy or compassion. To understand our attraction to violence and war, we must grasp that many social forces demand that we live with two faces, two personalities.

This book attempts to formulate a perspective on pacifism rooted in the authority of the Gospels. To the extent that we have public debate about war, that debate often focuses on just war theory. Just war theory has a long and honorable history, and it carries great weight. But it is far less useful than its advocates have supposed. To understand the virtues of pacifism, it is therefore important to see how flawed and contradictory are the tenets of classic just war theory.

Pacifists are often accused of being extremists because their accusers believe the pacifist position is a complete refusal to use violence in any circumstances. This is certainly the ideal. But it is hardly fair to the pacifist position to limit pacifism to this one extreme, though wise, position. No one would suggest that advocates of just war are people who think that all problems should be solved by nuclear attacks alone. Neither should pacifism be limited to a single choice in the face of conflict. Therefore this essay explores modified forms of pacifism that have been advocated and adopted over the centuries. These positions have great weaknesses, but a full exploration of pacifism needs to present and evaluate these alternatives. A recent Mennonite work, *At Peace and Unafraid*, explores the possibility of using nonlethal force and more broadly reflects on what has been called an "impasse" between classic pacifism and advocates of just police action. The alternatives considered here are limited to defensive force. Other contemporary authors, including Glen Stassen, have put forward a reformulated just war theory that articulates a series of admirable practices for peacemaking. His book makes a different suggestion, based on the conclusion that none of us is in a position to intervene in other cultures before we have addressed the log in our own eye, the severe shortcomings of our own societies.

This book ends where it begins. We are faced with a continuing human propensity to turn to violence that creates long-lasting conflicts among groups. Pacifism has value because it is the one approach to conflict realistic enough to understand that while nonviolent methods of change can be effective in the short term, as Gene Sharp has shown, the big conflicts of this world will take generations to resolve. Fast and violent solutions never accomplish anything more than temporary postponements of conflict. Because real solutions take generations to unfold, we must also recognize that we are not called on to have the answers. Rather, we are called to hunger for righteousness and to go about the work of making peace with the right tools and in the right spirit. Other books on this subject make many concrete suggestions for ways communities can help to bring about peace in the world. Some of those suggestions include programs for making praiseworthy investments in education, health, conflict resolution, and other efforts. This book closes on a slightly different note to make the point that we may all profit from asking more deeply what we must do to correct our own culture before we ask what the world needs from us. Therefore this book ends by repeating one of the primary messages of the Beatitudes: We are not to assume that we know what is right. We are rather to begin our work with hunger and thirst for righteousness.

These chapters begin by defining the questions that pacifism must answer to be accepted as a vital and viable force in the world. The problem of our double existence is probed next, followed by an interpretation of the curious answers offered by Jesus in the Beatitudes. Two chapters then assess and reformulate just war theory. The conclusion proposes reasons for adopting pacifism as well as initial steps toward a pacifist approach to conflict.

Thomas Trzyna
Pentecost 2006

Introduction

Pacifism. An alternative to war, a methodology for change, a spiritual commitment. Pacifism arises repeatedly in history. Its successes have been notable, especially in the form of nonviolent methods for social change in such places as the United States, South Africa, India, and to a lesser extent in the Philippines and Eastern Europe, to cite some of the more prominent cases in just the twentieth century. Buddhist pacifism played an important role in Indian history. The teachings of Mo Tzu impacted China in the time of Confucius. However, the pacifist position always faces stern opposition for being weak or unrealistic. What is its basis in the Gospels? Can it be said to be the core of Jesus' teaching? How does it fare in comparison to the promises of just war theory and the purported successes of war? Does just war theory even stand under analysis, or does it contradict itself? What would a pacifist approach to conflict look like, and how would that approach systematically differ from the use of violence to confront social and political evils? Are there compromise pacifist positions? Is pacifism practical? And how would one start a practical pacifist program? All of these questions have been debated, but they are worth continued meditation because of the potentially dangerous conditions we ceaselessly create in the world. Moreover, pacifist teaching ultimately speaks to alternative ways to live and to understand one's own being in the world. This exploration addresses these questions within the framework of one central biblical text, the Beatitudes, as well as in a handful of closely related passages from the Sermon on the Mount. It is not designed to be a comprehensive scholarly review of an old and important subject, but rather to be a focused meditation on taking the first steps toward a pacifist way of life.

Pacifism is almost universally rejected. It is an elitist position, some argue, because it maintains a moral superiority to any other view. Of course, those who advocate war are just as ready to praise their own wisdom and courage when they argue that participating in war is necessary and therefore morally superior to pacifism. Pacifism is an unrealistic position, others say, because wars have always been necessary, just as police are necessary, and therefore anyone who holds a moral position so far out of whack with current reality must be a fool. And yet healthy governments and societies of all types initiate and carry through change without war, and police in many nations carry no lethal weapons. Or, some say, pacifism is not implied by anything in the Christian religious texts. After all, God is a God of war in the Old Testament. The prohibition against murder is just that, a prohibition against killing as murder, meaning a personally motivated choice to kill a neighbor. There is no biblical prohibition against killing in war, they would say. If the Old Testament wars are to be our model, however, do they provide a warrant for anything more than hand-to-hand combat with spears and swords? Why should advocates of war think that God commends bombers, cannons, or nuclear weapons? Further, say other critics of pacifism, what Jesus said about loving enemies was intended as a rhetorical challenge or as a code for the next world or as an exaggeration. He just wanted us to like our enemies. But Jesus returned to this topic repeatedly and taught that there was no merit in loving only those who love us. The heart of the change he called for was to rise to loving those who wish us harm.

As Albert Schweitzer wrote at the end of *The Quest for the Historical Jesus*, the world always reasserts its values. Trust the world to do that, to reduce any fresh idea or any profound assault on received wisdom to an affirmation of the status quo. And that, finally, is the kind of argument C. S. Lewis makes against pacifism in *The Weight of Glory*: The faith is not really over and against the world, but in conformity with the highest values of military civilizations. Jesus does not call us to try to create a different kind of world. He may have been wise, but his wisdom did not extend to articulating principles that might be used to make radical improvements in this existence. Jesus is not a worldly philosopher or a practical moralist. He is a divine figure who leads us toward another world, a man who has little continuing interest in the fate of this one.

Those who favor war believe sincerely that war has produced good. The twenty-five or fifty million dead of World War II were worth the price to defeat the evils of Nazism and Japanese expansion, they say. Advocates of war argue that the collapse of the Soviet Union and of Ferdinand Marcos's Philippine dictatorship were in part due to military threats, not to the exhaustion of hopelessly corrupt regimes and to the passive and courageous refusal of hundreds of thousands of people to continue to participate in business as usual.

Those who favor war, however, credit a merciful or forgiving or pacific philosophy for one idea: the importance of being dispassionate, the value of doing the work of the sword without emotional heat, so that the taint of death does not harm the character of the one who wields the sword. So we have philosophies of justice, like Bishop Butler's in the eighteenth century, that emphasize the virtue of serving as police, on juries, and in execution squads dispassionately, without personal engagement. According to this reasoning, what distinguishes a truly enlightened civilization from one less enlightened is that the hangman takes no pleasure in his work.

And yet in stark contradiction to this notion, most people are taught that criminals who kill in cold blood are the worst of all. Those who kill without passion are the kinds of criminals unworthy of any mercy whatsoever. In some cultures, a man who kills his wife or his wife's lover in the heat of the moment is excused. A crime of passion is an honorable and forgivable crime, while a calculated slaying to suppress a witness or a victim, done without passion, is considered horrific. How can both of these positions be true? How can passion be good in crime and evil in the pursuit of justice?

The underlying principle seems to be that whenever we kill, we must do so in a way that points the finger at some other person: If I kill in a moment of passion, I am acting out of my normal character and the circumstances excuse me. If I kill while on a jury or on the battlefield, I can point to the role I am playing and say that my role did the killing. Recently, this view has received confirmation from the public anger showered on a general in Iraq who admitted that his troops took pleasure in killing insurgents. Of course they do. Of course, having seen their friends killed, they are angry and take some compensatory delight in getting even. And yet we want to maintain the illusion that those who fight do so with a kind of zombie-like impartiality.

Under these contradictions lies a simple recognition that killing and violence are indeed wrong, that pacifism has a point after all, that the culture we have created over some thousands of years indeed leaves us tainted. Now, it may be true that what Jesus had in mind was an ethic for another world. It may be true that to read the Gospels as a map for a new world order may be wildly mistaken. Yet the exercise has been attempted, and some of the results have been striking and constructive. One can point to the names: King, Mandela, Gandhi, Dorothy Day, and many others. Surely the Gospels are more than a road map to heaven; surely they also have a message to carry concerning the proper conduct of the present state of affairs.

The famous practitioners of pacifism and nonviolent social change, however, have not necessarily laid out a full program of what may be the intent of the Gospels for social action. Moreover, history shows us that different advocates of nonviolent change have propounded quite distinct approaches. Central and South American liberation activists, like some of the early Anabaptist and nineteenth-century advocates of communal living, proposed Christian models of action that are very different from the techniques advocated by Thoreau, Gandhi, King, and others. The brief meditations of Lanza del Vasto, the student of Gandhi who took the Gospels as a basic manual for contemporary action, provide rules for engaging public issues through publicity and fasting, like that used by Cesar Chavez to assist Chicano and Chicana farm workers. Even though pacifist strategies have been developed before, the effort is worth making again to make the point that the Gospels are at their core a statement of pacifism rather than a philosophy that can be made to comport easily with the current demands of diplomats and generals. A study of the Gospels also helps us to gain a richer portrait of the ways in which they spell out a comprehensive pacifist worldview.

1
A Double Life

The common public understanding of violence requires everyone to live a double life. In his *Pensées*, Pascal's description of human diversions explores how industriously people slave to avoid being quiet and taking stock of their real situations. We say that we want to live at peace, and yet our actions show that we would prefer to experience the illusion of constant and even violent activity that appears to have some kind of objective, because moments of true peace are threatening. Peace brings us face to face with what we truly are. Peace offers us opportunities to make hard choices, to create rather than to consume, to take initiative rather than to follow familiar paths. Peace is a terrifying experience. Immanuel Kant wrote about activities that are purposive without purpose, that seem to have a direction without really having any. He had the arts in mind, because in an art form such as music, the activity consists of leaving and then returning to a dominant tone. Suspense and interest are created by the cleverness with which a composer delays the return and the number and complexity of variations the artist can introduce along the way. Increasingly, though, the cultures of the world are training us to find satisfying entertainment in those purposive activities that lead to deaths, either real or imagined.

The advent first of television and later of video games has exacerbated the extent to which people now lead double lives. Clint Eastwood's early film *Dirty Harry* offers the perfect prototype for the life that we increasingly live in our imaginations. That film was a Greek tragedy. As in *Oedipus Rex*, a "striker from afar" brought a plague on the city, except that in the modern version, one who strikes from a distance is not a plague but a sniper who wields a high-powered rifle. Vulnerable victims are chosen, particularly children who are sexually abused, tortured, and then killed. In other words, the story line focuses on the worst of crimes to make the point that by resolving this crime, all crimes can be solved in the same way.

This haunting film makes a point familiar to readers of anthropologist Rene Girard. Girard has argued that sacrificial rituals tend to focus on stories of the worst that people can do, such as cannibalism, incest, and child murder. Television now has brought this formula to primetime viewing with "special victims unit" dramas about sexual abuse, torture, and murder. Where the old formulaic mysteries of Agatha Christie portrayed victims as nasty people whom everyone wanted out of the world, the formula now calls for painful sacrifice of the virginal and innocent. In the Eastwood version, the hero is lamed by injuries, despised by the population, and ultimately required to give up his authority by throwing away his badge, just as Oedipus at the end is blind and led away from his kingdom. The detective serves as the scapegoat and takes punishment due from the lust for revenge we may have experienced during the film. The audience, however, is allowed to participate fully in the torture and death of the offender. And the audience can walk away from the theater without guilt.

We say that we would prefer to live in peace, but perhaps because we are surrounded by frustrations that we do not effectively express through conversation, debate, or creation, we settle for a nightly dose of Greek purgation ritual, if indeed these experiences purge us of anything. Recent studies of pornography demonstrate just the opposite. Quite contrary to what Aristotle preached, social science shows that our continual immersion in this kind of violence deadens our sensibilities and increases the probability that we will imitate what we see on screen.

Otherwise, we can be very passive. In ancient Greece the purgation rituals took place only twice a year, and public participation in political meetings was required. Now we participate less in public activities, according to many surveys, while we relish nightly doses of violent tragedy to the degree that one of those "purgation rituals," video gaming, has been defined as an addiction.

We have become, in the classical Greek sense of the word, idiots—those who do not participate as required in political life, those who hold back and live in private, those who take pleasure in the idiosyncratic. Is television an addiction too, like video gaming and gambling? The two faces of the mask we wear are more extreme than were the masks of the ancient world: one of our masks is more passive, the other more violent and demonic. In place of comedy and tragedy, we exhibit the faces of ennui on the one hand and of savagery on the other.

While violence and also sex require effort on our part, they are alluring precisely because their consummation does not require much skill or engagement with ultimate meaning. We surround marriage and relationships with rules, and likewise we have rules for the conduct of war. But sex and violence can be performed without training or forethought or attentiveness to technique. The lowest common denominator of behavior is what any idiot can do. In fact, such behavior is *all* an idiot can do, because an idiot has no social relations that allow him or her to consummate anything more complex than rape or a brute attack. The idiot who is inwardly passive and thoughtless dons a mask of lust or a mask of violence to enter the public world.

How difficult it is, by contrast, to pause for thirty minutes and think, to learn to paint a fresco that will add to the beauty of a city street or a building, to learn to play a musical instrument well, to engage in research or surgery or any art with passion and concentration. How difficult, too, to participate in public meetings, to enter the public space and play an active and constructive role in the making of society. How difficult not to wear a mask at all.

Peace is not the absence of war but a positive, carefully cultivated condition that providentially still dominates most human behavior. It is easy to overlook how pervasive and successful is peace, how much peace has extended its reign even as the power of violence and the addiction to violence have also grown. A stranger can be set down almost anywhere in the world and thrive, do business, carry on conversations, share perspectives, and all without being threatened or killed. Of course, exceptions exist, and we focus much of our media attention on those exceptions, because they are salted with the violence that attracts our interest. Though some places are fatally dangerous to any outside visitor, peace is the norm of existence, not just a series of brief periods between wars. Peace is the assumption that neighbors will act in predictable and constructive ways; that light will be shed on most activities so that we can understand and respond appropriately to what transpires around us; that conversation will continue in its normal, broken way; that somehow we will manage to communicate.

In the immediate wake of an event such as the 2005 bus and subway bombings in London, one impulse is to hunt the perpetrators and carry out the ritual of vengeance. How satisfying therefore to hear the British prime minister call for understanding of Muslim people. The first actions after such explosions of violence can be calls for hatred or instead visits to establish or maintain communication with those of a different faith or political persuasion.

If pacifism can offer no practical actions to take in the aftermath of such an event, it cannot be called a useful philosophy for this world, even as it remains a viable otherworldly perspective. Pacifism needs to offer an answer to this question: in what sense is "the manual," del Vasto's name for the Gospels, a document for moral action in daily life? How do the manual's prescriptions differ from those of any other ethical philosophy? Are the costs of those actions worth paying? How do they compare to the costs of other forms of moral action? It is therefore moving to see a major political leader take a pacific step in response to a national tragedy. Such an action underscores the point that our best responses, after all, are motions toward peace and understanding.

The standard for judging the effectiveness of pacifism should not be simply whether pacifism has a lower body count, say, than philosophies of retribution. One can argue that the Soviet Union collapsed of its own weight and finally because of the largely passive and to some extent religious nonparticipation of its citizens. If enough people echo Herman Melville's *Bartleby the Scrivener* and just say, "I prefer not to," then any system will slow to a stop eventually. One can by contrast argue that the Soviet Union collapsed because the Soviet treasury was exhausted by keeping up with the arms race and the cost of the proxy wars that the East and West staged in places such as Vietnam, the Congo, and Malaysia. To those who showcase World War II as the perfectly justified war, one might even argue that in the end the Third Reich would have collapsed for lack of a reason for existing—except to kill. What measuring stick can be used to settle such a debate? How could one ever know whether pacifist approaches would have cost less in the end?

We do know, however, that in many cases the "weapons" of medicine, communication, compassion, service, education, and trade accomplish what guns cannot. And yet pacifism will not win many adherents by making points in a direct comparison between the efficacy of war and the efficacy of peacemaking, because pacifism will seldom be able to make the case that its methods will succeed quickly. We always look for quick and easy solutions, and nothing is as fast as violence. After all, we measure violence in muzzle velocities and other statistics of explosiveness and immediately applied power. Pacifism, however, ought to be able at least to present a coherent theory that might stand side-by-side with the various just war theories, whether Augustine's or Grotius's, or other formulations.

In fact, just war theories stand in need of support from a theory of pacifism, because the just war questions, while helpful in any analysis of a war, ultimately fail. As Lanza del Vasto observed so well, "Of course war is just, because it is just on both sides." In other words, just-war rationales can be built equally well on both sides. One side may claim an immediate offense, such as an incursion across a national border, while the other offers a historical explanation of a prior claim to that land. One side defines last resort in terms of one set of negotiations and treaties; another cites a different set of precedents and principles. One side claims that the chosen methods of war are evil because they involve numerous civilian fatalities; the other side explains how well its weapons have been designed to target military "assets" and accuses the other of putting civilians in harm's way. At best, each side reports a score of four or five on the seven common standards for just war and then turns the theory into little more than a framework for publicity and propaganda.

Seldom is a war perfectly "justified," and in those areas of doubt the other side finds the materials to construct its own just war defense. Rarely if ever does an international discussion lift up the famous criteria as the official set of standards for debate and decision. For example, just war theory asks whether this war is a last resort, if every other alternative has been attempted. If pacifism has a role to play in international dialogue, where weapons are not likely to be laid aside any time soon, then pacifism should offer a coherent set of possibilities for avoiding the last resort and prescribing a set of activities for avoiding conflict. Obviously diplomacy and aid programs address this question. Does the manual provide any additional practical, moral, spiritual, or psychological resources? A later chapter addresses the just-war criteria in detail.

Pacifism needs also to be more than merely a statement of the horror of war and a refusal to engage in further war. Jean Giono, like other pacifists of the generation following World War I, makes the case that war is horrible, that it twists people into monsters. His and other works from the great literature of World War I also brilliantly and forcefully etch the message that war finally produces disgust and exhaustion.

Wars do not necessarily end because anyone has won. They often end because everyone has reached a state of apathy and exhaustion. Analysts of World War II sometimes ask why the Allied forces did not move more rapidly into Berlin or ensure the freedom of Eastern Europe, why Churchill and Roosevelt were willing to cede Eastern Europe to Stalin and to Communism at Yalta. The answer seems to have been a decision to stop when the first key goal was reached and to spend no more energy and personnel on further conflict. The war was won, but the war also ground to a halt, leaving a generation of Cold War to follow. Recently the generation-long war in the Sudan has come to another end—perhaps an end that will endure this time, unlike previous truces. No one has won. Both sides can be said to have given up after years of slaughter. Still, showing that war does not succeed very well does not make a strong case for pacifism. Those who find war necessary will always argue that it is a last resort, but a necessary one, because no other strategy will produce safety or the survival of a culture. Even when war produces stalemate and exhaustion, those sad results are better than defeat.

Giono and others, though, make an additional observation about war that should be emphasized: training for war and participation in war changes people. Training individuals to kill and to be part of "teams" takes away their normal moral autonomy. When a powerful authority teaches that it is proper to live a double life, with two simultaneous standards of morality, that teaching leaves a permanent impact on the way societies function. Without such training, it is hard to imagine that so many peacetime businesses and other institutions could insist that to be "professional" means to leave one's individual conscience at the door of the workplace and to adopt a second, corporate set of loyalties and morals while at work.

The warlike frame of mind helps to cultivate institutions in which people believe that moral standards are relative, that loyalty to the job means closing one's eyes to certain kinds of wrongdoing, that speaking honestly is bad form, that blowing the whistle is wrong and punishable. War may dehumanize people, but perhaps the more malign transformation brought about by the human commitment to war is the creation of institutionalized personalities that are numb, amoral, and without creativity. The issue here is not that people become one-dimensional, as philosopher Herbert

Marcuse argued, but rather that they learn to compartmentalize their experience so completely that they never seek to integrate themselves.

Within such a framework of thinking, perhaps one might view post-traumatic stress disorder as a kind of leaking of experience from one sealed area into other sealed compartments. The programming and the debriefing were not sufficient to build a strong enough container to hold and organize the experience of war. Yet even those who do not show stress have been damaged, because they have been inducted not merely into the military but also into a permanently double and fragmented life. Books like the British poet Edmund Blunden's *Undertones of War* hint at a level of damage still deeper. Blunden, who left Europe for a life in Hong Kong after World War I, writes so eerily and quietly about his four years of trench warfare—starting when he was a mere seventeen—that it seems he moves in a world filled with cotton wool, a world in which no sensory stimuli can reach him. A world of lingering neurasthenia.

Another aspect of this socialization is the way that wars gradually persuade a population that further conflict is the only way out. On the one hand, exhaustion and disgust set in; on the other, war seems to take away the tools to achieve any other kind of resolution. During the Vietnam War, one commonly expressed fear was that if the United States military withdrew at any time, there would be a bloodbath of retribution in Vietnam itself and also the immediate fall of other regional states into Chinese Communist forms of government. Neither happened. My translator and associate, on a recent trip to Vietnam, spoke soberly about his time in prison, about the discrimination he faced in schools because he was related to a leader of the South Vietnamese CIA who was indeed executed by the winning side. Another one of my associates spoke of his ten years of re-education in a prison because of his work as manager of an American air base during the war. They described the severe taxation of southern assets. Neither described the aftermath as a bloodbath in the sense of the Japanese occupation of Nanqing, or Pol Pot's elimination of the educated classes in Cambodia, or even Mao's slaughter of Kuomintang forces in Shanghai. The dominoes of the famous domino theory have not fallen. Vietnam fought China again in 1979; Laos continues its peculiar existence as home to a majority of ethnic Vietnamese, failed communist state, and drug haven. Meanwhile in Hanoi and Saigon (now Ho Chi Minh City) the expatriates return to help build a nation and to collaborate with their former enemies.

As the American intervention in Iraq continues, the same ideas circulate. Isn't a bloodbath inevitable if the various Sunni, Shia, and Kurdish groups are left to sort things out for themselves? Won't Saudi Arabia become a terrorist state (if it isn't already)? Won't Iran dominate the region? War becomes as addictive as methamphetamine or cocaine. Withdrawal in either case seems to be attended with death or terrible risks.

War has very little to recommend it, though human populations tend to adopt it not as a last resort, but as a relatively early strategy for gaining attention or producing changes in leadership. Most societies disregard how history teaches that the first steps into violence almost always lead to a morass that extends past the military action itself into racism and the creation of group hatreds. Above all, war leaves us with fractured people who live in states of double consciousness, praising peace but voting for military action.

In spite of this, withdrawal from war carries with it all the fears created by any change of place or culture. However terrible the landscape where you find yourself, it is hard to move and look for a new home. If post-traumatic stress is defined by inescapable memories of horror, perhaps the medical community should create a term for the syndrome that occurs during every war. As the U.S. Congress begins to confront the chaos we have exacerbated in the Middle East, the legislators have that same frozen look they manifested in the Vietnam years. They are trapped and undecided in the gray land between their divided selves.

Recent studies of forgiveness, another distinctive aspect of the manual, have moved toward the conclusion that forgiving is not limited to something that one does in response to a particular injury. Rather, if forgiveness is to be effective, it must be practiced daily as the face that one shows toward life. Forgiveness must be a combination of action and predisposition.

Pacifism, too, must be not merely a stubborn refusal to take up arms, but more importantly a disposition to act in such a way that peace is maximized. Because a pacifist approach to conflict is not likely to offer any quick solutions—anything as resounding as an explosion or the headlong, twirling impact of a bomb—pacifism must be a steady disposition and a constant work rather than a response like a fire engine that can be driven out of its garage when a conflagration has already started. Pacifism must begin with the resolve to live a single rather than a divided life.

2

The Manual
and Moral Progress

What, then, does the manual—the Gospels—offer? What positive case can pacifism make for itself? But why the manual? Two large religious traditions, Buddhism and Christianity, embrace a pacifist perspective at their beginnings. Baha'i, the Jain, and other smaller groups also affirm pacifism, and ancient Moism taught its own curious form of pacifism and self-defense. Each has produced its share of pacifist groups. In fact, Buddhist India produced a pacifist kingdom that lasted for a period, though its leader, Asoka, converted to Buddhism and pacifism after conquering his neighbors.

Those who claim that the Judeo-Christian tradition contributed unique insights to democracy must more adequately confront the pacifism at the root of Christianity. Those who argue that Jesus of Nazareth was a brilliant philosopher would be well served to find in his fragmentary sayings further bases for the development of a peaceful world society. Even from the Jeffersonian perspective that argues that Jesus is merely a wise man, there would be some intellectual benefit to explaining precisely what that wisdom is. Sadly, much that Jesus taught has been disregarded or called unrealistic by many writers over the centuries, particularly when his teachings have conflicted with the dominant legal and military ideologies. Forgive enemies? Forgive criminals? Turn the other cheek? What invitations to social chaos, they say.

The manual makes an additional, even unique, claim on our attention. Unlike the teachings of Buddha or Mo Tzu, the gospel is part of a religious philosophy that is distinctly committed to reaching out to serve others, to work for the least of these. Mo Tzu taught a kind of withdrawal similar to Swiss neutrality; Buddha taught compassion, but his work focused on retreating from the cycle of passion that dominates the world. Christianity teaches active engagement with the world, and so Christian pacifism, if it is useful or meaningful at all, ought to be able to make a strong case for attention, and beyond attention, for practice. We live increasingly in a world that makes few distinctions among religions, a world that tends to affirm the identity of all faiths. So it is important to note that Christianity makes truly distinct claims with respect to pacifism, forgiveness of enemies, and active engagement with the world's pain.

If one looks into the gospel accounts of Jesus' sayings with the convictions of a believer, one can take the manual as a prescription for the future world or as a group of hyperbolic statements meant to teach far less radical ideas. Those have been the positions of many Christians. But if one takes the manual seriously as a guide to improving the present world, one is left with the task of looking for insights that may not have been widely developed or at least not widely applied. At worst, a search for a more convincing pacifist philosophy in the Gospels could lead to assertions that they contain a secret meaning that has not been noticed. Claims of that sort are common enough in popular literature and ought to raise a great deal of skepticism.

No claim is made here for an unusual reading of the texts. There is value, however, in looking at Jesus' words as wisdom for this world and then attempting to organize these thoughts into a program for action. Such a program may or may not differ from programs proposed in the past. If the manual has a special claim on us, certainly it calls on us to persevere in the task of trying to make its messages real and tangible.

During the Reformation, pacifist groups in western and eastern Europe, some of which influenced English religious and political thinkers, created pacifist and communistic centers for living. Those groups (Anabaptists, Socinians, anti-trinitarians of various stripes) wrote extensively about the theories of their pacifism, and they struggled particularly with how to fit their ideas into a larger state structure. Many of them reached the conclusion that true Christians could not serve in any government capacity or use courts of law or use weapons under any circumstances whatever. Some of the early church fathers reached the same conclusions. Later, some of those groups temporized their views, but they did not attempt to articulate ideals for larger communities. They concluded, rather, that they would always need to live in isolation, as small sects merely tolerated by surrounding peoples. Moreover, they understood that they were likely to be tolerated particularly because they were peaceable, productive, and often willing to settle where others would not. But must pacifism speak only to small communities that set themselves apart?

Working Assumptions

As ground rules, this exploration begins with the following working assumptions. The manual is a guide for present living. It contains ideas that are worth reconsidering as approaches to creating a peaceful world. Those ideas may be applied to any size of community. The application of those ideas does not necessarily require isolation from the rest of the world. Any insights that emerge from thinking through the manual are likely to come from taking the set of ideas together rather than individually. The Beatitudes as a group are taken to articulate a systematic viewpoint.

All of these givens are subject to revision and debate. They are stated as givens not because they are demonstrably true, but because they define at the outset an intent to avoid at least some of the cul-de-sacs into which discussions of pacifism have been led. The whole set of ideas in the manual need to be considered together because one of the rhetorical strategies in discussions of war and peace has been for one side to find a single flaw in the other side and then walk away with a feeling of victory. To put it another way, attackers of pacifism tend to yield very little ground and consider the subject closed once a point or two have been scored. Usually, an opponent points out an example of pacifist "extremism" and the conversation ends.

Pointing to Stalin does not constitute a sufficient refutation of Marx. If you give no weight to Marx's analysis of labor conditions, poverty, and oppression because of twentieth-century totalitarian communism, you miss an important lesson about the way the world really works to produce suffering. Disparaging all the philosophical ideas of American conservatism because you dislike the policies of Ronald Reagan or George W. Bush is to deny yourself access to a significant body of thinking about values. Discussions of pacifism often begin and end with a version of the Hun-raping-your-grandmother scenario. What could a pacifist do on September 1, 1939? If pacifism cannot offer a convincing argument for that date, all of its claims are dismissed by its critics. To make that gesture of dismissal, however, is to miss some of the most important teaching of a prophet respected by every tradition. Moreover, to make any such gesture of dismissal on any topic is to join the ranks of the idiots, the ranks of those who have lost the ability to participate in public discourse.

Further, a fair comparison of any pacifist philosophy to a hawkish perspective ought to permit both sides some latitude in defining themselves. Pacifism is generally characterized as an extreme position—precisely and universally the commitment never to use violence under any circumstances. Such an extreme pacifism was the commitment made by the Dukhobors, who were persecuted by the Russian tsar and rescued by Leo Tolstoy at the end of the nineteenth century. Mohandas Gandhi nor Martin Luther King Jr. were not pacifists in this rigorous sense, because they held out the possibility of violence as a last resort. King's "Letter from a Birmingham Jail," for example, makes enough oblique references to Black Nationalism that readers could understand that behind the softer campaigns he led with the Southern Christian Leadership Conference lay the real possibility of armed resistance by groups such as the Nation of Islam and later the Black Panthers. Mohandas Gandhi explained to his student Lanza del Vasto, as reported in del Vasto's *Pilgrimage to the Sources*, that it was better in the end to fight than to be a coward if you had run out of all other alternatives. King and Gandhi therefore practiced what might be called a situational pacifism. It was their strategy of choice, but not their only position. The conversation about pacifism needs to honor such leaders as well as spokespersons for other, less rigorous pacifist philosophies. Lanza del Vasto's, for example, argued that in the truly last resort, even committed believers may cast aside what they believe in favor of immediate action against a dangerous enemy.

Those who advocate just war theory generally start with a belief that war is absolutely justifiable. They qualify and defend their position by drawing on criteria from just war theory. And they obtain a kind of moral credit for making gestures toward the theory, even though the theory itself is deeply flawed. Pacifists should be allowed a similar degree of latitude in the positions they take. Pacifists believe that war is not justifiable. Some, however, have entertained the possibility of justifying certain kinds of violence in unusual circumstances, and their positions are considered here.

Insofar as this book is a thought experiment, an exploration of the manual, it begins with an additional hypothesis: human moral progress is possible. Moreover, moral progress may involve the development of new institutions and the elucidation of new conclusions from our most honored texts. To say this is no more than to embrace what has been an assumption of the last two hundred plus years of western history. Fully traditional cultures hold that people ought to return to past moral and social practices, whether Sharia law or male-dominated marriages or secret societies. Traditionalists in the West have embraced this perspective, just as fundamentalist Muslims have. To the contrary, most thinkers in the West have asserted the possibility not only of scientific progress but also of moral progress, and on this ground western societies have argued for centuries that old social standards must be abandoned in favor of new truths in areas like slavery and women's rights. Baha'i has perhaps taken the most radical stand on this point, arguing that new revelations from God will over time bring new moral and social truths to the world, but only when the world is ready to receive them.

Ethical Assumptions

This particular book is grounded in a variety of ethical assumptions. Some weight is given to divine command theory, in the sense that the Gospels are taken to be a privileged text that has a divine origin. At the same time, it is assumed as a starting point that ethical principles of any type ought to have a practical value as judged by any secular audience. Pacifism ought to be an ethic that can be tried in the world and found widely useful and constructive. Of course, pacifism always has a special value for those who believe, as did monk and prolific writer Thomas Merton, that the person who spends a life in isolated and silent prayer is contributing more to the world than most who are actively living in the hurly-burly of commerce or politics. While many people might respect that view or even agree that such lives of prayer have a real effect on what transpires around us, few are willing either to practice accordingly or to cite such a position as evidence for the worldly value of peace or prayer.

Pacifism also has a special and rarely disputed value for those who believe in the efficacy of self-sacrifice and martyrdom. The present intent, however, is to seek whether there are strong reasons to adopt pacifism from a pragmatic perspective as well as from a divine command perspective. If human morality can in any sense change for the better, perhaps a fresh or slightly more persuasive formulation of pacifism may be one of those improvements.

Of course, moral progress is a controversial idea. If one starts with Hobbes' imaginary cave-man perspective, in which life is "nasty, brutish and short," then the introduction of just about any standard of moral conduct is an improvement. If the Enlightenment is chosen as a starting point—and there could be other starting points—then moral progress can be seen in the series of revolutions (bloody and bloodless) that brought about an increase in democracy, universal male suffrage, women's suffrage, other women's rights, labor unions and workers' rights, attention to the sufferings of working children, the abolition of slavery, the abolition of judicial torture in most of the West, improved prison conditions, rights for mental patients and the disabled, the freedom of colonized peoples, and other advances for some if not all of humanity.

The internalization of those values, the acculturation of

succeeding generations in those values, makes not only for progress in small details but also for the strengthening of such foundational principles as the equality of all persons, whatever their age, class, wealth, or gender. For some but not for all, the move toward additional rights for homosexuals constitutes a natural extension of this series of moral improvements. The idea of a war to end all wars once conveyed a similar belief that humanity had progressed to a point where war would no longer be necessary. More recently still, we have heard declarations of an end to world conflict.

John Stuart Mills' 1859 book *On Liberty* stands as one of the landmarks in this panorama of moral change. It also remains one of the more controversial assertions of moral progress because of his beliefs that there are victimless crimes (such as prostitution) and that people should have the right to fulfill themselves in any way they wish so long as they do not infringe on the rights of others. Mills' reasoning assaults the dominance of the community over the individual and likewise the dominance of traditional religious and social values over the creativity or the self-actualization of each person.

Important to keep in mind is simply this: whether one agrees or disagrees that public morality has changed, can change, or does or does not progress or improve in any sense, the belief in such change is deep in our current western civilization. Similarly, reaction against moral change is deep in western and other cultures in the form of various kinds of conservatism, traditionalism, and fundamentalism. No judgment of these views one way or the other is needed here. The point is that if moral change is part of world discussion, rightly or wrongly, then traditional pacifist views are as much entitled to serious consideration as any other views that present themselves as improvements either in the principles or in the application of moral philosophy. Moreover, to the extent that belief in moral change dominates popular culture, those who participate in that culture may have a responsibility to give ear to arguments for change in the direction of pacifism, just as they give ear to various fundamentalist and liberal assertions.

It may be that moral progress is as amenable to measurement as scientific progress. In the sciences, experiments are tried and repeated, some hypotheses are proven false, and others are at least temporarily enshrined as truths. Social changes are less carefully controlled, and yet the social sciences continually attempt to measure, isolate, and evaluate the consequences of changing values. Neither moral science, if there is such a thing, nor physical science has a clean record of demonstrated progress. No one debates the worth of the abolition of slavery or the discovery of penicillin. Few would find nothing controversial in the invention of napalm or the changing attitudes toward marriage and divorce.

Alternative Approaches

Evaluating pacifism may also require an approach that is different from evaluating war. The typical question to a pacifist is, "What would you do if a Hun were raping your grandmother?" Del Vasto's response to this sort of question is to say that under certain extreme circumstances, anyone of any belief system is likely to default to some form of violence, even if it is preventive violence rather than intent to kill. This kind of question constitutes stacking the deck. A more appropriate question for anyone, pacifist or just-war advocate, might be this: what would you propose to do in the face of people who always wanted more?

In the film noir classic *Key Largo*, Humphrey Bogart, playing a World War II veteran, asks a gangster played by Edward G. Robinson just what it is that he wants out of life. The gangster speaks for the acquisitive aspect of all humanity when he replies with just that one word: "More." That word implies a weird form of arrogance; it says, "I am immortal, and therefore I will have time to use all that I acquire." "More" says that I have persuaded myself that I am not this mortal individual, but rather I am capable of living an alternative life that is grander, longer, more important than any normal human lifespan. I have at any rate a mask that allows me to pretend that I am immortal, and when I wear that mask, I want more of everything.

One of the problems with an anti-pacifist perspective, which is another way of stating the norm, is that it entails precisely this kind of commitment to "more." How many weapon systems are enough? How many simultaneous wars must one be able to wage, even when there is no other superpower left? Why indeed do these purchases of equipment rank higher in national priorities than education, transportation, aid, and other efforts to address the causes of conflict? If "more" is a cause of violence and conflict, then the solution will not come in the form of an action that can be taken instantaneously, such as seizing property. The peaceful response will take longer. So if the question "What would you do if . . . ?" is posed with the tacit addition "What would you do instantaneously to fix this problem?" then pacifism will fall short, just as war falls short when one looks at its results over the long haul.

Pacifism also offers a different answer to the question, "What is the ultimate goal of resolving conflict?" Just war theory, as it is applied in actual practice, begins with the assumption that what is to be protected is some not-fully-explained social system that has a right to maintain its identity. That system might be defined as "our way of life" or "our nation" or "our civilization" or perhaps merely as "our territorial integrity." America waged the first Iraq war to defend the territorial integrity of Kuwait and its form of monarchy.

No one suggested that the conquest of Kuwait by Iraq, after the initial horrors of rape and pillage, was actually going to lead to an end of the Kuwaiti way of life. Under Iraqi rule, Kuwaitis could continue to practice Islam and live within the framework of Islamic and Arab civilization.

Still, the justification for the first Iraq war differed very markedly from the justification for defeating Nazi Germany, where there existed additional threats to civilization, including the potential for the extermination of all Jews, Poles, Gypsies, homosexuals, the disabled and mentally ill, as well as a potential for the replacement of Christian civilization (roughly speaking) with some newly invented form of pagan totalitarianism based on Norse or Teutonic mythology.

Just war theory is lacking because it does not raise this very fundamental question about the nature of the threat to the ideas and the basis of civilization. Christian pacifism begins at this earlier point by articulating a series of convictions about the nature of the good society, the society that is worth building by peaceful means. These convictions include many that secular people choose not to accept. The Dukhobors whom Tolstoy helped to rescue from Russian persecution did not particularly care if they all died. They believed that it was their responsibility to be fully pacifist and that God would lift up other believers in other communities if all the members of their sect disappeared. This extreme example makes a simple point: the conditions under which Christians are prepared to live, should they accept a strict reading of the Gospels, may be far more difficult than those others would accept. Where others would feel pushed past the last resort of negotiation, pacifist communities might just accept those conditions as part of the task they are given to work with in their ministry.

The manual, then, has as much right to be considered seriously as any other social philosophy. It makes distinct claims that are quite different from those proposed by other religions, even other pacifist traditions. The manual may lead to additional moral progress in this world. At the same time, it asks us to reconsider what our goals in life ought to be: whether we are to be focused on ourselves or on others, whether we are to live as one person or behind several masks, and whether our lives are to be defined by a lust for "more."

What then does the manual have to say about a pacifist worldview? What do the first Beatitudes teach?

3

What the First Beatitudes Teach

When Lanza del Vasto wrote about "the manual," he had in mind particularly the Sermon on the Mount, of which the Beatitudes form an especially challenging section. Translations of these texts vary considerably. One of the more recent English translations, like earlier French translations, opens each of the Beatitudes with the phrase "Happy are they" rather than "Blessed are they." *Blessed* is an odd word that suggests saintliness or perhaps moral goodness. In English it probably derives from *blooded*, so that it brings to mind the Passover and the salvation of the people through blood sacrifice. But it also suggests that the condition of being blessed is to be bloodied in some sense, as in "bloodied but unbowed."

Happiness is an equally odd concept. Americans are accustomed to thinking about *happiness* in its eighteenth-century meanings. The word became very popular in that period as people began to imagine the possibilities that opened to them as a consequence of new freedoms. Jefferson of course substituted *happiness* for Locke's *property* in the phrase "life, liberty and the pursuit of property." We look for life, liberty, and the pursuit of happiness. Something that makes you blessed, then, might produce giddiness, spiritual exaltation, bloody complicity in a hard work or suffering for a worthy cause or moral worth, or perhaps just contentment. Alternatively, blessedness may be a kind of perfection, to the extent that any human conduct or character can be perfected. "Blessed are they" could also be reduced to a simple meaning such as "it's a good thing to . . ."

The whole complex of meanings, however, takes one straight into the dark heart of religion—that place where sacrifice, awe, gladness, participation in something important, moral value, and many other ideas are mixed with bloodiness, pain, commitment, work, and loss. So one might conclude that "blessed are those" means "if you want to get to the core of things, then this is how you ought to act." Jesus' words in the Beatitudes, like many of his parables, are suggestive rather than explicit in their meaning. His sayings are in this way similar to Buddha's parables. However, the two men are very different, because Jesus was teaching something to be applied in society, whereas Buddha taught chiefly a philosophy of personal retreat. The comparison is worth making here because many of us have now been exposed to Buddhist texts, and we are accustomed to the oblique way in which they teach. Jesus in the Beatitudes, like Buddha in many of his parables, is describing indirectly what it is like to be in a condition of happiness or blessedness. Happiness or blessedness is like nirvana. It's like something, but he can't precisely describe it because it has no real meaning or feeling until you have experienced it. Moreover, the experience is paradoxical to the point of being contradictory because, as the mere word *bless* indicates, the state is one in which happiness and bloodiness find their union.

One might stop here and say, of course, that's just ordinary theology of the crucifixion. But that is not the direction this exploration is taking. That high theological road can lead to treating the text as one that describes another world or that concerns a moral order that has no immediate role in the governance of the world. The issue here is what the manual tells us to do now. What does Jesus say in the Beatitudes?

Why start with the Beatitudes? Because they present in a particularly crystalline form a summary of Jesus' teachings. Why begin with an assumption that they posit a pacifist worldview? One might answer this by citing Jesus' words about turning the other cheek. Or with del Vasto's observation that Jesus was not teaching passivity but rather offering a practical insight that most people (except utterly evil ones) will think twice before hitting you again. During that moment when the aggressor takes stock, there is an opportunity for moral growth. Anyone who slugs you once in passion, you hope will think before hitting you again and choose not to do so.

Perhaps this is what Jesus had in mind also in one of the more peculiar sayings that appear in the apocryphal Gospel of Thomas. There he is reported to have said something like this: "You wouldn't stick a sword into someone before you had stuck a sword into a wall and twisted it to see how it felt." After working out anger on the wall and understanding the damage that can be done with a blade, perhaps you would choose not to stab at all.

Of course, Jesus also remarks that he came not to bring peace but a sword. There he may speak precisely to our double consciousness, which needs to be broken down so that we can live as complete persons with one rather than several masters, one rather than several moral codes, just one face rather than two.

These are fundamentally pacifist teachings. They direct an avoidance of violence and an embrace of self-criticism and rationality. These examples also demonstrate the pragmatism and deep wisdom of what Jesus taught. His words invite us to look further for additional and equally practical wisdom. However one looks at these aphorisms, they speak about a worldview dedicated to peace. Therefore one test of the assumption that Jesus taught pacifism is to look to the philosophy of the Beatitudes and ask what kind of moral and political views those statements undergird.

No doubt the Sermon on the Mount was compiled from many sources and speeches, though the long and traditional assemblage of those texts gives an authority to them as a coherent statement of a religious and moral philosophy. This book assumes the Sermon is a coherent unit and that the advice about turning the cheek flows from a set of general principles.

The collection of sayings called the Beatitudes holds a preeminent place within the Sermon on the Mount. They constitute from an intellectual standpoint a very high level and abstract group of assertions about the nature of a perfected (blessed) religious life and the blessed (blooded) path that wends toward that life. Moreover, the Beatitudes come to us in a particular order that hints at a logical sequence: from most basic principle, to applications of the principle, and then to consequences and encouragement. Other interpretations are certainly possible, but this is the one that serves as the foundation of this essay.

Within a short scope, the Beatitudes and the verses that close them contain twelve strange assertions. These twelve might be set side-by-side with other codes that operate at a lower ethical level. The contrast demonstrates just how extraordinary the Beatitudes are in their complexity and depth. The Ten Commandments, for example, outline principles that we may violate, but that are not subject to much debate either as to their legitimacy or as to the difficulty of understanding them. Aristotle's *Ethics* emphasize moderation and fitting into the social structure. The eightfold path of Buddhism emphasizes self-control. Confucian principles focus on self-control, obedience to the hierarchy, and moderation. The Boy Scout oath, which encapsulates a set of Confucian-like principles for British and American culture, can be reduced to obedience and above all to the kind of dual existence that is consistent with war and with corporate conformity. All of these codes are relatively transparent in their messages.

The Beatitudes, by contrast, boil down to praise for a kind of world that humankind has seldom experienced. They speak of emptiness, grief, gentleness, obedience to God, and a will to console others. They tell us to be merciful when we have power to do otherwise, to seek purity of heart (whatever that may mean), to work for peace, to accept persecution, to expect to be cursed and abused, to be willing to be lied about, to understand that our life will be corrosive to others, and to seek the ability to shine light into dark places. Above all, the Beatitudes describe a way of being in the world that emphasizes emptiness, anticipation, and readiness.

Most of these statements are framed not as duties to be performed but rather as reactions to anticipate. If you do as you ought, whatever God requires of you, expect to be cursed, abused, lied about. Expect to be irritating to others. Expect to be in uncomfortable places and to experience grief. Expect to be empty, whether that means powerless or without answers or without tools to work. The world's other great moral codes are more similar to the Book of Tao in that they help the practitioner to be like water, to fit in, to flow above or through conflict. They are guides for "making it" or at a minimum guides to "getting by without being noticed" in the world as we know it. Other groups of aphorisms also offer advice on how to achieve religious mastery: to become a Confucian great man, to reach Nibbana, to unite with Brahman, to be popular or successful.

In a wildly contrary way, the Beatitudes contain nothing beatific or beautiful: they invite conflict and failure rather than explain how to achieve success and *savoir-faire*. They do, however, describe a life of courage. Certainly it requires great courage of one kind to fight in a war and to expose oneself to sudden and painful death. By way of compensation, military training offers a discipline for coping through conforming oneself to a prescribed set of behaviors that entail becoming welded to a group of individuals who share the same training and ideals. Through this training, one gains a separate and second identity that shields one's civilian identity. To put it differently, you are filled by the training. Filled with ideologies, drills, a new identity as part of a group, slogans and songs, and activities to fill the days.

The Beatitudes begin with an emptying that is more severe than the Buddhist program for controlling desire. They offer no promise of mastery. The courage they require is courage to be exercised while feeling empty, not filled with a dogma or a set of nationalistic beliefs.

The first Beatitude, the first foundation of the pacifist religious philosophy, is that you will be happy, you will be following the right road, you will be a peacemaker, if you recognize, know, and accept your own emptiness. Meekness and humility are, after all, kinds of emptiness. To be meek or humble means that one does not claim knowledge, power, or standing. *Blessed are the poor in spirit, for theirs is the kingdom of heaven.* Those who know themselves to be empty will inherit the kingdom. Empty of what?

Jesus' first and foundational comment summarizes a vast quantity of religious and philosophical thinking. The human existential situation, the condition of just being in this world, can be approached full or empty. You can approach life full of knowledge, answers, hypotheses, strategies, and certainties that you can impose on experience to force it to reveal predictable and familiar meanings. Or you can approach life with the understanding that you are fundamentally impaired in your ability to know anything at all.

Desiderius Erasmus wrote during the Reformation about the comic nature of Christianity. A Christian must accept that his or her wisdom is foolishness. Centuries before Erasmus, the long series of literary and religious works that come to us from the grail quest legends made a similar point. What sets the true grail knight apart from others is the capacity to ask naïve questions—above all the question, "What is going on here?"

Those who approach conflicts and opportunities empty are able to sit and listen to what others have to say about the issues and the possible solutions. Empty people do not bring canned solutions or panaceas. Emptiness of this kind is precisely what people in developing countries prefer from experts—the capacity to listen attentively to what people on the ground think about their own needs, whether they are right or wrong. Empty people do not offer remedies and interpretations before they know the cultures into which they step. Western literature presents this kind of emptiness both in the tales of those grail knights, who achieve the quest, and in the figures of comic characters who bring wisdom to chaos precisely because, like village fools, they can ask utterly obvious questions. *Candide* fits this mold; so does Grimmelshausen's *Simplicius Simplicissimus* (that most simple of all simpletons); so do various characters in the long picaro tradition that includes Lazarillo de Tormes and Cervantes.

The empty one has sometimes, not always, the capacity to deflate arrogance and to lead others to ask why in the world they would ever want to do what they had contemplated doing some minutes ago. These are also the people who exhibit childlike delight in almost any situation, which suggests that the promised kingdom of heaven is something that only a childlike individual can understand after all.

In what sense is this emptiness consistent with a pacifist ideology? Those who wage war are seldom empty in this sense. They take pride in having an answer as well as pride in the righteousness of their position. It is hard to make the Beatitudes' kind of humility consistent with just war theory, which is predicated on the belief that it is possible to answer questions, among them: What will guarantee sufficient noncombatant immunity? When have we reached the "last resort"? What are just goals for a war? When are the means of warfare just?

Sometimes generals too reach a condition of emptiness. The U.S. general who commanded the firebombing of Tokyo, Curtis LeMay, showed a curious kind of sobriety and self-reflection when he explained that if his side had lost the war, he would have been judged a war criminal. One hundred thousand civilians died in one night during that raid. To put the case positively, the posture of emptiness is one in which an opponent is not threatened with either weapons or assertions of righteousness. Instead, as in the advice to turn the other cheek, all sides have a chance to sit down and consider alternatives.

Honor is often cited as a reason for violence. Honor can imply an appropriate and measured sense of worth, or it can mean an exaggerated sense of worth brought about by putting on an institutional mask of one kind or another: racial honor, national honor, the honor of the organization, the honor of the tribe.

So-called "honor rape" offers an excellent case study of the way that honor of this kind, as contrasted to humility, leads to violence. Pakistani and Afghan tribesmen use honor rape as a method of justice. If a family has been dishonored because one of its women has been seen in public with a male from another tribe, then it is the duty of the woman's family to seek retribution. The punishment may involve gang raping a woman from the other tribe, or even gang raping or killing the woman who had the original conversation. Under the normal moral code, public chatting with women, extramarital sexuality, and rape are all utterly forbidden. But under the guise of protecting honor, men may be called on to assume the institutional mask and commit an abhorrent act that would be otherwise forbidden.

The only antidote to this dual existence seems to be a commitment both to humbly living as one is, with one face not two, and a further commitment to egalitarianism that flows naturally from the conviction that one shares a condition of ignorance and limited worth with all others.

The second Beatitude builds on this picture of negotiation grounded in what might be called a justly low sense of personal worth. *Blessed are those who mourn, for they will be comforted.* Mourning or grieving includes anger, at least so death and dying theorists such as Elisabeth Kübler-Ross maintain. What Jesus had in mind may have been limited to sorrow. Sorrow in the face of what we have failed to do or of what we have done wrong is consistent with the deepest form of humility and emptiness.

Mourning, however, is yet another peculiar term. Often the word is heard in the phrase "public mourning," which is one of those complex activities like a president's or a pope's apology for a historic wrong. Public mourning is not the same as personal mourning. In fact, public mourning can be used to set the stage for public hostilities. In the wake of a great public disaster, such as in the case of the 2001 terrorist attacks, the rhetoric and ceremony of mourning can be used to signal renewed public solidarity, singleness of purpose, or preparation for revenge. Media coverage of Islamic funeral processions also often carries this message explicitly. Today we steel ourselves and bury the innocent martyrs. Tomorrow we seek our revenge and strike the guilty murderers.

This second beatitude gains interest because of the way that "mourning" is paired with "consolation." If the phrase had been, "Happy are those who mourn, for they shall be satisfied," then clearly the kind of mourning Jesus had in mind would be consistent with girding up one's loins or preparing to take action. Consolation, by contrast, suggests that God will bring a resolution to feelings of grief or will offer a sense of deep meaning. Consolation is not an act you can perform for yourself, like seeking satisfaction. It is something that must come to you from without or gradually from within your own being. It cannot be made to happen.

Within the past two years, American public dialogue has produced sharp disagreements about the appropriateness of certain types of open mourning. These disagreements point powerfully to the different political and social uses to which mourning can be put. When a television network proposed to show for an entire silent program the pictures of soldiers killed in Iraq, some stations refused to carry the show on the grounds that such a display necessarily constituted an anti-war statement. The implication is that long periods of mourning, a lengthy and sober assessment of the cost and consequence of war, must necessarily be pacifist, whereas shorter coverage of military honors and remembrances are considered to be appropriate mourning that is consistent with a renewed resolve to fight.

A second implication is that to look at the individual faces of real people, as opposed to symbolic representations of "our boys," strips away the mask of military service and reveals the true human cost. Showing real faces breaks the rules for wearing masks. The Vietnam War Memorial in Washington, D.C., has produced marked responses of this kind. For similar reasons, a photographer was fired for taking and publishing pictures of coffins flown back to the

United States from Iraq. Anything that rendered the deaths personal and individual, any presentation that suggested the possibility that the deaths were tragic or a waste, was not to be permitted.

So if the end of mourning is consolation and reflection, then mourning is potentially pacifist; if the object of mourning is to gather up strength to carry on, then mourning becomes part of the rhetoric of war. Truly ambiguous cases include the choice to print photographs and biographies of the individual victims of the terrorist attack of 9/11. Did personalizing the victims produce simple empathy and grief, or did it incite a will to respond? Only a sociological study could begin to answer such a question. Perhaps the deepest difficulty with showing the faces of soldiers who have sacrificed their lives, to restate a point, is that it violates the first condition of modern warfare: that the soldier must wear a mask. To show the true face points directly to the underlying duality, the underlying distortion of reality on which military training and war are based.

Further, when mourning is for "the honored dead" as a category, then it is likely to be part of a public rhetoric of resolution. That, after all, is how Lincoln made the case in the Gettysburg Address that from these honored dead we take increased resolve that they shall not have died in vain. Americans were to maintain their resolve to win that war. To contemplate individuals, to mourn for real human persons rather than for abstractions like the unknown soldier or the "they" who "shall not have died in vain" or "the honored dead," is a different and personal form of mourning rather than participation in a public ritual.

The second Beatitude appears to ask us to mourn personally, for persons, not masks, and to do so with a hope of being consoled rather than satisfied or revenged.

A short anecdote helps to reinforce the point. During

the Korean War, a decorated World War II pilot gladly flew dangerous low-altitude support missions. But when he was asked to do high-altitude bombing of North Korean cities, he refused. He insisted that he had to see his targets. He said that he could not be an anonymous agent striking from afar, that he could not in conscience drop bombs that might hit civilian targets. He insisted on doing his best to guarantee noncombatant immunity, as specified by just war theory. His was a curious and courageous form of selective objection. Because of his record, he was merely denied further promotion and posted to kitchen duties. He refused to wear a mask.

The third Beatitude presents an interesting paradox. *Blessed are the meek, for they will inherit the earth.* "It's not the earth the meek inherit, it's the dirt," sang Mordred, the arch villain in the musical *Camelot*. The meek are the mousy, the timid, those who routinely submit to anything, the cowardly. No doubt Jesus had something else in mind by the gentleness that will be recompensed with a gift of the land that God has promised.

Taoist wisdom comes to mind here: those who are like water will survive because they will flow inconspicuously around all obstacles. More importantly, those who are like water will gradually erode obstacles. How long, precisely, is a reasonable time to wait for peace? For how long is a gentle approach to conflict to be allowed its small successes and losses, its progress, and its backsliding? On what kind of timeline would it be appropriate to plan for peace in, say, Northern Ireland, Rwanda, or the former Yugoslavia? Clearly force is not going to bring about the necessary cultural changes to lead people in such areas to live in harmony and mutual esteem together, Catholics and Protestants, Muslims and Orthodox Christians, Hutu and Tutsi. The Peace Corps was created with this kind of wisdom, the knowledge that it was likely to take generations of careful work by enthusiastic, generous, and even naïve young and older people to bring about gradual change in places where elders, diplomats, world bankers, and generals were distrusted, if not despised. Government structures are not designed to permit this kind of planning, the kind that develops a one-hundred-year blueprint (or more appropriately rough sketch) for the gradual pacification and resocialization of contested territory. At best, governments think in units of four or ten years.

The United States still suffers from real divisions between the North and the South nearly 150 years after the Civil War. Yet all the evidence suggests that it takes at least that long to begin to bring closure to such deep wounds. During the last few years, grand juries in some southern states have finally brought charges in cases like the bombing of the Birmingham, Alabama, church where four little girls died and the 1964 execution murders of Andrew Goodman, James Chaney, and Michael Schwerner, three civil-rights workers in Mississippi. Still more recently, a district attorney has reportedly started looking into the deaths of two black men whose bodies were found while federal teams were looking for the three civil-rights workers. The deaths of these two men had not even merited an investigation, but now the case is being pursued more than four decades later.

Forty years appears to be the amount of time necessary for the land to be reborn or to be even partially repossessed by a spirit of peace and reconciliation, and such is the time scale of racial reconciliation, the time scale necessary for ordinary people to find the courage and sense the conditions to be safe enough to poke into the darkest recesses of the past. Jesus' words here suggest that a true pacifist methodology must include planning for the very long view. The gentle of this generation may inherit nothing but the satisfaction of their good work, while another generation may inherit a land blessed with peace.

The absolute opposite of this view is the often-expressed sentiment that we can once and for all put an end to . . . whatever it is that irritates us. Or that we can have peace in our time. Or that the evil empire can be defeated now. Or that we can bring an end to history, insofar as history is a record of division and conflict. Or on a smaller scale, and more recently, that the Sunni and Shia and Kurdish people of Iraq would meet an invading American army with flowers and gestures of thanks. All of these claims have been made with undue optimism in the relatively recent past.

Pacifism seems to call for the realization that in any successful world future, discussions need to be held concerning what might be done over periods of fifty years or more to resolve even small conflicts. Judgments about the effectiveness of initiatives also need to be made over long periods. Trial programs of one or two or five years are not likely to be sufficient to make progress against problems that in the human course of events are likely to take five or ten or twenty decades to fix. Therefore any audience ought to be deeply concerned if not alarmed when a mere human politician proposes that any public evil with a long human history can be resolved, expunged, or defeated in short order.

The American recovery from human slavery offers an example of how long it takes to make progress. To quote Martin Luther King Jr., a "reluctant president" issued the Emancipation Proclamation well into the Civil War and that document had little immediate effect in either the South or the border states. In the upper North, free blacks still contended with fewer civil rights, and though in the period immediately after the end of the war, black Americans could boast even a U.S. Senator, Jim Crow laws quickly reestablished white hegemony.

As noted above, forty years after the Civil Rights Movement of the 1950s and 1960s, there finally has been partial closure on a few of the most notorious violent incidents of those years. More than forty years passed before the men who bombed the church in Birmingham were tried. That is sometimes how long it takes, a generation or more, before such events can be addressed even partially in the United States. Moreover, the process of creating a single society continues with constant disputes, test cases, recriminations, claims, and accommodations.

Recently, at least one journalist, Jonathan Kozol, has suggested that our nation is now sliding back into segregation or, worse still, apartheid. Little we have tried since the U.S. Supreme Court's Brown v. Board of Education decision in 1954 has evened the educational opportunities of black and white children in America.

What is a reasonable timescale for addressing similar issues, such as the near slavery in which the Berber half of the population of Mauritania keeps the Bantu half and the nearly equivalent condition of the "ignoble" half of the Niger people, who are dominated by the "nobles"? How long will it take for the Hutu and the Tutsi of Rwanda to overcome a history of domination and slaughter that dates far into the precolonial past?

Blessed are the meek, for they will inherit the earth. Which earth? Is this an apocalyptic vision that promises that the meek shall inherit what is left over when violence has done its worst and only ruins remain? Or do the words imply that a peaceful wisdom will ultimately prevail? Or does Jesus offer practical wisdom for these middle times, the big "in the meantime" in which we live without any immediate expectation of a second coming? This "meantime"

in which gentle negotiation may in fact be a more successful method than confrontation and invasion? Whatever the
scope of the recommendation, it is a recommendation for a
gentle strategy in the face of conflict.

4

The Final Beatitudes

The first Beatitudes paint the characteristics that are required by the life of engagement. The later Beatitudes focus instead on actions that one can take and the challenging results to anticipate.

As advice about a pacific approach to resolving conflict, the fourth Beatitude comports well with the third while adding another level of intellectual and spiritual complexity. *Blessed are those who hunger and thirst for righteousness, for they will be filled.* Or perhaps a better gloss on the words is this: blessed are those who seek to do God's will, for they will be filled.

The operative words here seem to be *hunger* and *satiety*. Earlier promises in the Beatitudes do not offer anything approaching satisfaction. Yet here too, in the fourth principle, the words embody complex meanings. It is not clear what it means to hunger for justice or righteousness or to receive satisfaction. Jesus does not assert that those who hunger for righteousness know what justice might be. He does not suggest that anyone seek to create justice. Rather he asks that those who would do God's will hunger deeply for what is right and to know God's will.

Earlier Beatitudes warn against arrogance, against knowing the answers and attempting to apply them. Here, the follower is asked to listen and wait to hear what is right. If an empty person enters a place of conflict with a will to seek what is righteous, will that produce the promised satisfaction? This is a mandate to work slowly and gingerly to seek solutions in which the satisfaction may be that an answer emerges or may be limited to knowing that one has gone about the work in the right way, with the right heart or hunger.

It does not seem possible to read this Beatitude as an invitation to take any stronger action. The person of good will is not invited to implement what he or she thinks is God's will, but to ask to know God's will. Nor is there an invitation to reach conclusions about which are the just solutions, but only to hunger for them. Permissible action is once again limited to what the grail knight must do in the face of his most difficult quest. The actions required are to be present, to recognize that something is amiss without fully understanding what is wrong or why, and to ask what is going on, so that conversation may begin. Finding the grail is therefore a bit like naming the elephant in the room or perhaps just noticing that something very large and unnamable is present. The quest truly demands courage, though no violence is required.

Some of the peace work in Northern Ireland has taken this approach. Peace dialogues have been carried out for years without an expectation that they would produce immediate results. In some cases, the work has continued in the face of outbursts of violence. At best, those who have committed themselves to the work have gained some limited degree of respect from the warring parties, and they have begun to educate others about what peace might be like.

Martin Luther King Jr. laid out four steps for a nonviolent campaign in his "Letter from a Birmingham Jail": determining the facts, negotiating, self-purification, and direct action. In his campaigns, the facts were often clear, though negotiation sometimes revealed new dimensions to issues and uncovered both new opponents and unexpected supporters. Clear facts included such realities as separate seating on buses, the lack of service in restaurants and hotels, and lack of jobs, for example.

In many conflicts, though, the "facts" are less clear. In the Middle East, for example, the current boundaries of nations were laid down quickly after World War I. Arabs feel a permanent grievance because they were promised freedom if they fought on the Allied side. But the French and British secretly concluded the Picot-Sykes Agreement, agreeing to hold on to the most attractive sections of Arabia for themselves: Palestine, Lebanon, Syria. And of course both before and after that critical time, there have been layers upon layers of additional facts. The division between Shia and Sunni goes back to the first generation of Islam, for example. So excavating the "truth" about such a place is like digging up the ancient city of Troy, with its seven or nine layers of settlement.

The anti-war protestors in the United States who followed in King's wake sometimes jumped from discussing the facts to direct action. They did not stop to negotiate or to purify their motives. As a result, some of their campaigns looked more like violent disruptions than attempts to reach understanding or to create positive change.

The Beatitudes lay a heavy emphasis on the difficulty of knowing the facts, seeking guidance, entering into dialogue, and remaining aware of one's own emptiness. Self-purification is another way of saying how important it is to identify and eliminate arrogance and illusions about having ready-made answers.

Some of the Irish peace workers exude this kind of expectancy that coexists with only limited hope for changes in the near future. *Hunger* is a good word for this expectancy. Hunger can persist for a long time and in the past was almost a daily experience. There is an Anglo-Saxon concept that combines the moral and the physical aspects of hunger:

agen-bite, or self-gnawing. One of the older English spiritual manuals is simply called agen-bite of inwit: the self-biting of conscience. The phrase suggests how moral hunger must be a desire for solutions to problems out in the world and at the same time a recognition that the same hunger for righteousness will lead to the self-eating that is conscience and self-examination. Hunger is a self-gnawing experience.

To hunger for righteousness has one further implication. It is a clear alternative to hungering for "more." Hungering for righteousness sets a very full and a very filling agenda, and in those senses hunger itself is guaranteed to bring satisfaction, though not the kind of false satiety one gets from "more" or from the short-lived rush of taking out anger against something. No one is truly likely to enjoy the smell of napalm or burned flesh the morning after. Hunger is instead filling in the sense that it focuses attention on the task at hand. Cesar Chavez's hunger strikes had that effect on others; so did the fasts of Lanza del Vasto and his companions, who in the late 1950s and early 1960s used hunger to draw attention to nuclear weapons and to the horror of French torture in Algeria, and who in 1957 published "An Appeal to the Conscience of the French" to announce the reasons for their first fasts.

The next Beatitude carries a different rhetorical force. *Blessed are the merciful, for they will receive mercy.* To the degree that these short and enigmatic phrases suggest trade-offs or even contracts, this Beatitude reads like the passage in the Lord's Prayer, "Forgive us our sins as we forgive those who sin against us." The implication is that we will be forgiven, or that we will be treated mercifully, if and only if we offer forgiveness or mercy. At an extreme, one might even read these phrases as saying, God will make an effort to help you, but only if you first try to conform to his will. This powerful phrasing suggests that among the Beatitudes this statement carries particular importance, a force that can be compared to several similarly extreme statements in the Gospels: If someone slaps you, turn the other cheek, and if you say "fool" to anyone, you will be judged.

All of these four statements on mercy, forgiveness, angry words, and submission to violence point toward the same two messages. First, not only is violence unacceptable, but any speech or action that promotes violence is profoundly sinful. Second, every measure must be taken to stop the cycle of violence and revenge, even if that means offering either forgiveness or mercy under the most challenging circumstances. It is worth accepting far less than "justice," for in any case we must ask whether anyone is entitled to justice in the eyes of God. Moreover, if swallowing some hurt and acting in humility will help to change the offender and to prevent further violence, why not make the attempt?

Forgiveness has been the subject of a significant amount of writing and research over the past three decades, with some of that writing focusing on distinctions between forgiving, mercy, amnesty, and other forms of traveling out of the thicket of conflict. In the past, philosophers, theologians, and political thinkers discouraged these actions for two reasons: they give away something that might have been claimed, and they may encourage further crime. More recently, writers have recognized a third and radically different objection to forgiveness and mercy. Forgiving is dangerous because the person who forgives or grants amnesty or chooses to be merciful places himself or herself in a position of moral superiority. Forgiveness, too, can be a judgment. And superiority of any kind constitutes arrogance that can lead to a renewal of the cycle of violence. How dare he forgive me, when he also has done so much evil!

It follows that mercy and forgiveness must be offered with humility, with emptiness of spirit, rather than with ostentation. This is a lesson that the wisdom of the world continues to resist. We want what is owed to us. We want "more."

On the other hand, forgiving and mercy can be understood to reflect no more than common sense, or perhaps inspired wisdom like Jesus' command to turn the other cheek. You turn the other cheek so that the offender has a chance to rethink his or her actions. Similarly, forgiving or being merciful is wise because peaceful accommodation is where you hope to end up in the long run. So you may as well save yourself the expense of conflict by moving as early as you can to the most satisfying resolution you can imagine. If this seems paradoxical, consider that at the end of most wars, if not all, the people involved in the combat must eventually return to living with one another in some kind of harmony, even if that harmony has its dissonances. Seldom does a war involve complete genocide. The Hutu and Tutsi peoples of Rwanda have tumbled into at least two major periods of genocide since the end of the colonial era. Neither community is extinct; neither group has chosen to leave the country. They must eventually find a *modus vivendi*.

Of course, regions such as Northern Ireland and the Balkans offer evidence that disputes and mutual slaughter can continue for hundreds of years, and the African conflicts that are more public now have had histories that extend deep into the precolonial past. Anthropologists can indeed point to cases of genocide where communities have destroyed each other or where a clan or sectional feud within a single tribal community has literally left only one man standing at the end. Claude Levi-Strauss described one in *Tristes Tropiques*, for example. Perhaps the Maya destroyed themselves in this way, as the most recent archaeological evidence suggests. One group killed all the inhabitants of a huge city and simply left the bodies to be discovered all these centuries later.

Extreme outcomes appear to be just that, however, extreme and unusual. The norm is continuation of conflict, with cycles not only of violence but also of peace and peacemaking. What Jesus points to is a simple idea: if in the end, to quote a line from a poem by Auden, "we must love one another or die," or at least put up with one another or die, then why not start now rather than later?

Moreover, ethnic conflicts tend to continue precisely in those places where "war" as it is generally conceived cannot offer any form of solution whatsoever because the parties involved choose to fight guerilla or urban conflicts and because they will not accept any stable national leadership that speaks with authority. The Beatitudes here speak to a very common and dangerous kind of conflict, a kind that can produce very large wars, but curiously a kind that does not fit the formulae of just war theory. Just war theory is predicated on the notion that there are organized governments who lead opposing forces. To put it bluntly, just war theory assumes that there are people in charge. Urban or rural internecine warfare and the policing activities that keep a lid on such warfare seem to call for a different theory and a different practice because the decisions to fight emerge inchoately from deep in the culture and from dozens if not hundreds of different cells of combatants. These groups are particularly sensitive to any reprisal that continues what they perceive to be the pattern of abuse.

So mercy, amnesty, and forgiveness have a potential to address the deepest source of violence. Whenever a leader says, in response to an act of violence, that the act was done by a person or group that did not represent the whole, whenever a leader makes a point that most members of a group are honored, then this is precisely the kind of mercy and understanding that can bring some degree of peace. Sometimes in such situations, leaders extend to the other side more credit than is due. If a prime minister says that he knows that most Muslims or most Serbs or most Irish Catholics or most Irish Protestants would never condone whatever it is that just happened, listeners may be entitled to some degree of skepticism. The rhetorical point of such a statement is to extend, even to overextend, mercy and understanding in order to produce peace.

Less difficult examples would be World War II and the Vietnam War. In whatever senses they were won or lost, both led eventually to periods of rebuilding, renewed communication among the combatants, and gradually improving relations. Not all of the guilty were identified, tried, or punished. Jesus' commands to be forgiving and merciful make plain sense because he asks that we pay a small price in pride rather than a large price in warfare in order to get to the same place: mercy, amnesty, communication, rebuilding, new communities. Besides, the small price we think we pay in working toward settlement is never exactly what we think it is. Those to whom we yield are expecting far more from us as the "justice" that is due to them. So those on the other side are not likely to read any sacrifice as a gift or a mercy that humiliates the one who offers it.

To return to an earlier example, a British Muslim who is treated to public respect and recognition, and who is not blamed as a member of his or her community for a bombing, may at some point have felt angry enough, victimized enough by discrimination, to have condoned a bombing. That individual may respond to any public "mercy" (in the sense of more than is due to him) with a feeling that any recognition is too little, given the daily insults and suspicion he or she must endure. Still, the empathy of the prime minister may have a positive effect, and for that reason if no other mercy and generosity are good public policy. As in the case of the other recommended behaviors, double consciousness or wearing an institutional mask is the chief enemy of mercy.

It takes extraordinary arrogance to think that the next war is going to have an outcome any different from the thousands of others that have preceded it. It takes a similar degree of self-delusion to think that one is sufficiently different from all other humans, sufficiently immortal or powerful, that this military attack or occupation will have an effect more significant or more lasting than any other.

Pacifism asks that everyone take a long view and consider how things are likely to look in fifty years or even in five years. Mercy too asks us to consider what kind of treatment is likely to produce the better long-term outcome. Even if the Nazis could have built "a thousand-year Reich," that time frame pales in comparison to the true length of history. Even if history could be brought to an end, one still would have to look into the faces and the neighborhoods of those who bore the price of such a victory. Recognizing that the outcomes of war will not differ, one can then try the alternative. One can short-circuit the ritual of war and go straight to the gestures of reconciliation, the accommodations, the acts of mercy, the issuing of amnesties, the exchanges of mutual forgiveness, the continuing conversations, the negotiations.

To teach mercy is not to ask anyone to accept less than is due. To teach mercy is not to suggest that anyone accept a lesser outcome. To require mercy means to mandate the strategy that will most certainly produce both justice and satisfaction. And therefore to teach mercy and to act mercifully is likely to produce an outcome in which all sides will in fact receive and maintain more than they ever expected, starting with the blessing of not wasting human lives and scarce resources on the hecatombs of war.

While the Beatitudes constitute a practical philosophy of pacifism, they also must be read in several other lights. The statements become more extreme and demanding as the sequence moves toward its conclusion. Any listener must consider whether the demands are moving into the realm of what is impossible to men but possible only with God's help. Are the conditions described even credible? The command to be merciful turns an action that is often considered a gesture of supererogation, something beyond justice, into the foundation that makes any form of justice possible. The next Beatitude, similarly, offers a hyperbolic statement that on closer inspection contains equally practical advice about creating the conditions for peace.

Blessed are the pure in heart, for they will see God. If pure means sinless, then this sentence refers to no one, and it explains why no one is in the habit of seeing God face to face. If pure, however, means unadulterated, single, homogenous, of one nature or personality, then the sentence asks for an action that flows naturally from all of the previous statements. Be one person. Not "to thine own self be true," because one's self might be corrupt. But rather, be one person who is humble and complete, who lives without masks. If you take off the mask of your role or your station in life, then God also will reveal his nature. From this point, the statements describe more graphically the nature of the life that can be expected if one makes a commitment to creating peace.

"Blessed are the pure in heart" may also imply what we know to be true in any case, that those who are pure in heart and who act out of these principles are not likely to last long on this earth. Whistleblowers will be miserable. Those who speak truth to power will die. The old saw of Renaissance poetry was that those who die young must have been closer to God, so he spared them the travails of a long life and old age. The pure in heart may go first to God because they will be killed.

This too is the wisdom of the next Beatitude. *Blessed are the peacemakers, for they will be called children of God.* Perhaps this is hardly reassuring, really, since the Son of God was crucified. Nevertheless, those who seek peace can expect to be both wounded—bloodied—and filled by their work. The verses that follow offer a picture of what can be expected not merely as a consequence of living up to the first Beatitudes, but also what one can expect to experience during the work of peacemaking: *Blessed are those who are persecuted for righteousness' sake, for theirs is the kingdom of heaven.* You will be persecuted, cursed, and abused. People will lie about you, and your only immediate consolation will be the knowledge that all peacemakers before you have suffered the same fate.

Other people are also cursed and abused, so just being cursed and persecuted is not necessarily a sign that you are doing good work. However, if you are working hard in a humble way to produce peace, and you are still abused, perhaps that is an indication that you are making progress or at least traveling along the right road. Someone at least is paying enough attention to be troubled by what you are attempting. Conversely, the passage suggests that if the world speaks well of you, there is reason to wonder if you are still having a meaningful effect. What could be more sorrowful than such predictions? So the philosophy of peace that Jesus articulates is recursive in the sense that its later propositions echo the earlier ones. Blessed are those who mourn, for they shall be filled. Those who do good work will certainly mourn.

Oddly, the world has a special place in its heart for great peacemakers, and so at a superficial level it would seem that Jesus' words are false. After all, he is widely respected. He is held up as a standard even by leaders of other religions. So too are figures such as Mohandas Gandhi, Nelson Mandela and Desmond Tutu. So was Martin Luther King Jr. among many parts of the American population, so long as he stayed out of the North, limited his concerns to segregation, and kept out of the politics of the Vietnam War. Peacemakers who continue to be an irritant, peacemakers who do not re-tire or who do not accept the role of senior statespersons, tend still to be killed or cursed. And once they are dead, the peacemakers can be redefined, just as Jesus' pacifism has been redefined to fit any variety of war-making.

Before leaders such as Tutu, Mandela, and Stephen Biko and the people of South Africa had brought an end to the apartheid regime, Tutu once visited a Seattle cathe-dral where he rebuked the congregation for failing to bring their Bibles to church. Though the congregation was pre-pared to applaud him as a courageous leader for freedom in South Africa, hardly anyone shook his hand on the way out, because he had dared to point out the congregation's own weakness.

What this says, of course, is that just as many ordinary people are expected to live a double life, with both personal and institutional faces, so too peacemakers are acceptable to the degree that they permit themselves to be cast in a double role. They are honored insofar as they speak about peace as something already victoriously won that we can celebrate as part of our glorious past or as something that will be won in the other world. They continue to be dishonored insofar as they continue to point out injustice, hypocrisy, and suffer-ing. They are noble when their actions bring to light prob-lems far away from us; they are an odious nuisance when they point out our own sins. Prophets are dishonored in their own countries, to be sure. They are equally dishonored away from home when they dare to speak too much truth.

To put this in another way that points to an important dimension of the issue of war and peace, great peacemakers please us to the extent that they seem to stand outside of time and make few immediate demands on us, besides our approbation. When peacemakers insist on touching our actions, when they insist on acting in the same time in which we live, we often find them obnoxious.

What may trouble us most is that peacemakers bring to bear a different understanding of time than the one with which we normally live. Violence as a solution to conflict is almost always predicated on the belief that actions taken quickly and forcefully can have a lasting effect. We persuade ourselves that "a lasting effect" of two months, a year, or five or ten years, is truly lasting. We talk about solutions of that kind as if they were permanent, even for all time. We use phrases like "once and for all" when it is delusional to think we have done anything that can last forever.

Peacemakers insist, to the contrary, that time is very long indeed, and eternity still different. Again, that is where the Beatitudes begin, not with a statement about time, but rather with a related assertion that we must be humble because we are more ignorant than we can possibly recognize. We cannot imagine what is likely to be known or said or done fifty years past the hour of our deaths. War is wrong because war misjudges time. War is wrong because it almost always is based on a false understanding of how long the present "solution" will last.

The verses of the manual that follow the Beatitudes speak directly to the ways in which peacemakers are irritants. Salt corrodes. The role of the salt of the earth is not to be flavorful, but to irritate, erode, oxidize, etch, burn, get at the core of things. Likewise, the role of light is to shine into dark places. Perhaps we would prefer salt to be the natural flavor of all the good things that we have earned. And light ought to be a star that shines pleasantly at a distance, out somewhere in the galaxies where it can have little bearing on our lives. But no, if we are to be salt, it is to be salt that penetrates. If we are to be light, we are to be light that shines where there is none.

Later in the Sermon on the Mount, Jesus reinforces his pacifist message with several equally memorable aphorisms. He counsels turning the other cheek, points out that there is little virtue in merely loving your friends, commands active love for enemies, and warns sternly against anger and cursing. Hard as his advice may be to follow, it amounts to a mandate to approach adversaries with humility, active love, and a willingness to suffer in order to bring about a semblance of justice and, above all, a condition of peace. Eventually mutual forgiveness and reconciliation may come, but we are not to expect them. We are to expect the worst.

Can this collection of aphorisms be anything other than a call to pacifism as a way of life that is both spiritually and morally correct? Is it not at the same time an eminently practical program for improving the conditions where we must live? Or do we truly prefer that other version of the Beatitudes by which we sometimes appear to live? Often it seems as if the world's set of "blessed" reads like this:

> Blessed are the gifted, for they shall have all the answers.
>
> Blessed are those who rejoice, for they need no comfort.
>
> Blessed are the self-assured, for they shall fill the libraries and the halls of state.
>
> Blessed are those who know what is right, for they shall impose it on others.
>
> Blessed are those who judge, for they shall obtain the

judgment they seek.

Blessed are the pure in intellect, for they shall grasp the end of all knowledge.

Blessed are those who fight in my name, for they shall be called Sons of Thunder.

Blessed are those who root out injustices in my name, for theirs is the kingdom of earth.

Blessed are you when people respect you and recite all kinds of praise about you on your own account.

Rejoice and be glad, for your reward is great on earth, for so men have respected the leaders and teachers who came before you.

You are the salt of the earth, and you have retained your savor.

The earth glitters with the crystals of your wisdom and follows your steps forever.

But this is exactly what Jesus did not say.

As a philosophy of conflict resolution, the pacifism described in the manual calls for empty and humble individuals to grieve over the wrongs of all people, to console and communicate with all parties, and to follow a practice of mercy and forgiveness whenever they have the power to act. Peacemakers are to suffer and to accept less than what the world considers justice, if worldly justice is defined as leveling the field or offering restitution equivalent to whatever has been suffered. Peacemakers should extend mercy and forgiveness to bring about reconciliation of warring parties with the understanding that justice will never be perceived the same way on both sides. Therefore those who have power ought to give a little more and take a little less in order to show goodwill and create the impression of justice on the other side, even if that means making a sacrifice.

Equally important, the manual requires that people get

in the habit of telling the truth to themselves about who they are and what they desire. We are to live one life rather than two or three, wear one face rather than several masks. Immanuel Kant's curious little essay "Perpetual Peace" came to a similar conclusion. Essential to peace were leaders who would be transparent, who would speak the same words in public that they voiced to their private advisers.

Contrary to the conclusions of those Reformation pacifists and early Christians that holding offices of power was inconsistent with the faith, the Beatitude that speaks of mercy suggests that it is appropriate for believers to serve in positions of power where they have the ability to be merciful. It is possible to read the Beatitudes as a code of moral conduct for those who separate themselves from the world. But to take that position reduces the words of Jesus to advice for interpersonal relationships. When Lanzo del Vasto asked a Vatican official how the Sermon on the Mount was to be applied in the world, that is the response he received: that Jesus merely made some moral recommendations that did not need to be followed and that in any case they applied to interpersonal relations within the community, not to larger issues such as nuclear warfare or rearmament.

The form of pacifism recommended here may appear to have value only if people are willing to think on the very long term, with the intent to begin processes of communication that will have an effect in ten or fifty years. But in the short term, this kind of pacifist perspective can serve a critically important role simply by making the point that real change must be expected to take time and effort.

The front pages of our newspapers are full of evidence that quick fixes do not work. Recently, we have been told that the people of Iraq would greet American troops with flowers and smiles. When that did not happen, there was no plan for even the next few months, much less the next five or twenty years. On the other hand, because we do not think about the long term, headlines about the warming of the seas, the melting of the icebergs, the disappearance of atmospheric shielding are all welcomed, it seems, in the spirit that those events do not matter yet.

The manual provides a blueprint for a life of constant engagement with public issues. In *The Human Condition*, Hannah Arendt credited Jesus of Nazareth with the discovery of forgiveness and also argued that a key social problem in the modern world was the loss of the agora. We have lost not only the skills to speak in the public square but also the sense that it is our duty to participate, to be a member of society, rather than an idiot. The manual calls for dialogue and participation in public life to the end of preventing crises that produce violence. Yet the manual offers more than just a superb method for achieving peace. It also complements the most popular just war theories by providing a framework for addressing what kinds of conflicts are really worth being considered as "last resort." And when the axioms of the manual are set beside a careful understanding of just war theory, it is also apparent that while classic just war theory offers an interesting and useful set of questions for analyzing conflicts, it is a less useful strategy in the face of violence than is pacifism, for just war theory is riddled with contradictions and difficulties of application.

5

Just War?

Just war theory is a set of moral guidelines that has not been made law in any arena. It generally includes eight principles: last resort, just cause, just ends, limited objective, just means, limited means, noncombatant immunity, and a reasonable chance of success. What the public sees of just war theory, on the rare occasions when it is discussed in the press, is a set of philosophical ideas that are usually invoked *after* the fact, as justification, rather than *before* a war, as a system for decision making. Through most of this discussion, the criterion of last resort is bundled with considerations of a just cause.

Sadly, just as Americans know little of the Bill of Rights and the U.S. Constitution, they know even less about theories of war. As with Martin Luther King Jr.'s four steps for nonviolent campaigns, the Geneva Conventions, or the Universal Declaration of Human Rights, the media have not striven to educate people in the history of the church's just war theory. (Surely such foundational sets of ideas are as important as the food pyramid or the recommended daily allowance of vitamins!) Pundits occasionally make reference to the theory, but usually implicitly rather than explicitly. Academics from Mennonite or Catholic traditions make reference to it but do not commonly address it in high school or college education. How much curricular space do we spend on formal ethics of any kind? A theory that is not part of public culture is not likely to have much value in guiding public discourse. So as a "theory" or a "set of principles," just war theory is bankrupt from the start because it fails in two fundamental ways: it does not define what is worth fighting about, and it is not part of the public consciousness or the body of law.

The same could be said for the Beatitudes, of course. We have public debates about placing the Ten Commandments in public buildings. Those commandments share content with the codes of other early civilizations. Many of the principles are in fact enshrined in laws against murder, theft, and adultery. So it is difficult to understand why they are controversial, except for the fact that they are quoted from the Bible. Imagine how the contemporary American public would respond to public display of the Beatitudes, with their far more radical ethical content!

The first and most critical limitation of just war theory is that it does not define the kind of war that is worth justifying. All of the criteria for just war are subject to debate and interpretation, which is why Lanza del Vasto so wisely remarked, "Of course war is just, it is just on both sides." Seldom does a war meet all the criteria, and often those on both sides of a war can tout a similar "score" of just-war criteria they can satisfy.

After the Gulf War, a number of Christian and other writers weighed that conflict using the criteria and debating their scores. For some commentators, America and her allies could tout a score of four out of seven, a simple majority, though nothing in the theory indicates what should be considered a good-enough score. The cause was reasonably just and the objectives were limited: returning Kuwaiti autonomy. The chance of success was high, and the chance of a negotiated settlement negligible (Kuwait had already been invaded). On the other hand, the means were not limited to endangering the troops, but also included significant damage to the infrastructure of Iraq. Noncombatants were killed in large numbers. The means were of questionable justice and humanity. American forces used depleted uranium shells, and when the Iraqi army was in clear retreat, allied aircraft employed carpet bombing against the escaping troops.

The Iraqi government, on the other hand, was able to argue that its cause was just, because Kuwait was historically part of Iraq. The invasion was quick and targeted, ensuring success and a limited use of means. The means were generally just, because no dirty weapons were used in that particular attack. There was no chance of a negotiated settlement by which the Kuwaiti royalty would surrender their sovereignty. Moreover, the goal was well defined. Unfortunately many noncombatants were killed. That's a score of six out of seven.

Del Vasto's insight proves true. What good is a theory that both sides can use equally well? What kind of theory is this, in fact? The term *theory* as applied to the justification of war suggests several meanings. The theory is theoretical in the sad sense that it is not universally practiced. Is it possible to find a series of wars that have been prevented because the theory was applied and discussed? Or a series of wars in which one side agreed that its case was less just?

Second, it is a theory in the sense that it is a framework of principles that can be tried in the court of public opinion and used to define what is just. Lawyers often use competing legal theories to try complex cases, citing different precedents as well as different logical arguments.

Just war theory has no greater standing than any other theory of politics. Consider the criteria individually.

Just causes are often defined in terms of some obvious wrong, such as a breach of territory that cannot be resolved within a particular period of time through negotiation. Two cases may cast some light on the difficulties of deciding when a wrong is sufficient to justify military action. During the American Civil War, tensions ran high between the United States and England because of British support for the Confederacy. British traders ran blockades to continue the cotton traffic and to supply the Confederate States of America. At the other end of the United States, as far away from the battles of the Civil War as can be imagined, the United States and Britain waged a phony war over what each took to be potentially a just cause for military action. Known as the Pig War, this conflict developed because of an ambiguity in the treaty that defined the new border between the United States and British Canadian territory.

Vancouver Island was British. Oregon territory was American. But where was the line to be drawn with respect to the flotilla of little islands that fill the strait between Vancouver Island and what is now Washington State? Would the five or six habitable islands known now as the American San Juans be Canadian or American? Citizens from both nations occupied the islands. Real territory was at stake, and hence there was a justifiable cause for war if no settlement could be reached. Armed units from both nations occupied San Juan Island, and one armed party killed a pig belonging to the other side. That was the only casualty of the war. No one was killed. Indeed some later famous warriors participated in the occupation, including Henry Roberts of Robert's Rules of Order, who built the miserable American bunker in a site exposed to the worst of the region's weather, while the British more wisely built their camp, complete with a formal garden, in a well-protected inlet.

While this is a silly example, it allows an important point to manifest itself. Neither British nor American rule over the San Juans was likely to change any aspect of the lives of the people who had settled the islands. Either way, the citizens would have the same rights to religion and freedom of speech, similar governments, elections, free trade, assistance with development, and access to services such as mail and police protection. Native peoples who visited the islands could expect about the same treatment from both nations. Neither nation intended to use the islands as a base for invasion. If the two nations' pride had not been engaged on another matter, no one would have thought twice about simply allowing the issue to be settled quickly by some minor bureaucrats. Does this really meet the standard of a just cause?

Similarly, when the United States purchased a slice of Mexico to complement Arizona, the Gadsden Purchase, legend says that the surveyors who were drawing the border got tired and took a northerly slanting path toward water and a known city rather than a straight line across to the sea. If they had done their work as originally planned, they would have hit salt water at the Gulf of California, and as a consequence all of Baja California would be part of the United States. The difference was not worth debating at the time nor in the context of already difficult U.S.-Mexican relations, so the border stayed as surveyed. The cause, if it was one, was not sufficient. In legal terms, it was *de minimus*: too small to bother with.

In the case of the Pig War, however, no less an authority than German emperor Kaiser Wilhelm came out to visit the San Juans and make a ruling. On the face of the original treaty, the British may have had the fairer claim to the islands; the fact that the emperor gave them to the United States may have had more to do with German-British competition than with the justice of the American cause. What was gained?

Some other recent wars have had "just causes" of this type—causes that were not sufficient to justify an hour's thought but proved sufficient to take away many human lives. Peru and Ecuador, for example, got into a tiff over a stretch of desert on their border at a time when Ecuador was bankrupt and Peru struggling with the Shining Path movement and a failing government.

In the case of the Gulf War, in which Kuwaitis indeed had a just cause because their nation had been overrun by the Iraqi army, the Iraqis committed many crimes against the Kuwaiti people. Most commentators have agreed that these injustices constituted a sufficient cause for war, and that there was no option other than a violent response. War was in fact the last and only resort. Even in this apparently perfect case, as will appear later, there may be reasons to question whether there was sufficient justification for military action. Assessments of this war have tended to focus not on the justice of the cause, but rather on a series of issues related to the other just-war criteria. For example, were Colin Powell and President Bush smart to limit the war to the initial objective, the restoration of Kuwaiti territory, rather than to use the opportunity to topple Saddam Hussein? Were the United States and its allies justified in bombing Baghdad or in carpet bombing the Iraqi army as it retreated from Kuwait, thereby inflicting tens of thousands of additional fatalities on a force that was running away? Was there any attempt to guarantee noncombatant immunity or were the allied forces too cavalier about accepting "collateral damage" during the war and during the sanctions that followed, which caused tens of thousands of civilian deaths due to poor nutrition and inadequate access to medications?

Suppose, however, one were to consider the possibility that the restoration of Kuwaiti sovereignty was not a sufficient justification at all? While this is a controversial suggestion, wouldn't most of the world have accepted it if the United States had not chosen to lead the intervention?

There were justifications, of course. The just reasons include the ethical mandates to restore land and government. The less just reasons involve the politics of oil and the murky business of supporting a congeries of less-than-moral governments throughout the region, including extensive past support for Saddam Hussein in his wars against Iran. In spite of these justifications, it looked at the time as if many European and other nations were prepared to accept Iraqi control of Kuwait. Why?

As in the case of the Pig War, whether the Iraqi Baath Party or Kuwaiti royalty controlled Kuwait, the people would have experienced nearly the same rights to religion, legal redress, and conditions of life. Iraqi plutocrats would have ruled rather than Kuwaiti ones. These two examples, in other words, begin to ask the question, Just how deep does a justification have to be to justify a war? In both the case of the Pig War and the Gulf War, there was a clear violation of national sovereignty. In the case of Kuwait, there were clear violations of personal rights, personal property, and life. Yet in neither case was there a threat to a civilization or to a way of life in the sense that Nazism threatened the continued existence of western-style democracy with Judeo-Christian ethical foundations. The greatest danger if Kuwait became part of Iraq was rather to the continued rule of U.S. ally Saudi Arabia, an undemocratic state.

And yet that is not the end of the tale. In the case of the Gulf War, a slightly deeper assessment of justice might have looked at one of the world's most horrifying statistics. Many nations have populations that are evenly divided between men and women. Some states, like the Baltic nations, have far more women than men. Others, such as the Arabian nations and the Gulf states, have significant "deficits" of females. Media have often covered the crime of female infanticide in China, especially under the old one-family, one-child rule. And wife murder and female infanticide are still common enough in India to produce a slight imbalance of the genders. In China, as of 2005, there were 106 men for every hundred women. In India, the ratio was 105 to 100. In the Gulf, however, the most recent statistics include these: for every 100 women, there are 150 men in Kuwait, 117 men in Saudi Arabia, 128 in Oman, 214 in the United Arab Emirates. These are places with longstanding disparities of gender and patterns of limiting educational and other opportunities to women.

Some of these gender differences may be explained by the importation of male laborers to support these economies, but women are also imported to do domestic work. So there is reason to believe that sexual discrimination is a significant problem in many of these nations. Secular Iraq did not and does not number among the nations that have imbalanced populations with respect to gender. At first glance, it seems that America went into the Gulf War to preserve a regime that in at least one important area was far less preferable to the Iraqi dictatorship of Saddam Hussein.

A third recent example of a war that had only a superficial justification is the Falklands War, where Britain acted precipitously to seize back the Falkland Islands and their sheep from an Argentine invasion. The failing and morally disgusting Argentine regime, which had carried out a secret war against its citizens, meant to make a point for itself against an old colonial power. Britain rose to the bait, and rather than waiting for negotiations or using other less lethal methods of warfare, played at gunboat diplomacy. While the war was a victory for the ghostly remnant of the British Empire, no one would suggest that the price in ships, men, and treasure was worth it. The cause was arguably just, in the sense that the British had occupied the islands for a long time, but was it sufficient on either side to justify the carnage? Where was a sense of proportion? The fact that the war helped to bring an end to an odious Argentine regime is beside the point. More tragic is the fact that the world had done so little by way of exerting pressure to end that government and its secret executions and torture years before.

These examples help to define what may be the most important practical limit to pacifism, though it is a limit that extreme pacifists would not accept. An extreme pacifist holds that the only source of value is faith, and therefore it matters little whether the whole world be destroyed, so long as faith be maintained. An extreme pacifist would hold that should God choose to continue a faith, it will appear whether in death camps, gulags, or any other setting. It is not the Christian believer's duty to guarantee social or political conditions under which religious practice is possible.

There are religions, of course, that hold a different view. Zoroastrians believe that in the ultimate conflict between Ahura Mazda, the god of light, and Ahrahman, the god of darkness, human conduct will tip the balance one way or another. Hence it is important for there to be Zoroastrians (Parsees) to continue the faith. A little differently, some Hasidic Jews believe that the Messiah will come if all Jews obey the Law.

Nothing in a Christian understanding of the world requires believers to act in a particular way to bring about the second coming and the day of judgment. Those events are out of human control and known to God alone.

A less extreme Christian pacifist might compromise a little, out of a kind of moral weakness or perhaps a moral "realism." On such a view, a person who was primarily committed to pacifist solutions might under extraordinary circumstances choose to enter into combat because he or she was convinced that the very continuation of faith on this earth was in danger. And even though God was to be trusted in such a case, the believer could not resist the urge to fight with weapons rather than to trust that God would bring about better times or whatever in fact constituted God's will.

The nineteenth-century Russian pacifist Leo Tolstoy explores a related idea with respect to the justification of war in his epic *War and Peace.* He portrays Prince Andrei Bolkonsky, on the night before the Battle of Borodino, expressing the following thought: If there is to be a battle and all the wisdom of the world is to be cast away in favor of having a bloodbath in which over a hundred thousand men are likely to die, then let there be no pretense, no double-consciousness, no rules about how war is to be conducted. Once you make the choice to stage a battle, why not announce that it will be to the utter death—no hostages, no mercy, no temperance—just blood and death. Let there be no rules of war.

Tolstoy uses Kutuzov, the Russian commander-in-chief, to portray the opposing view. Yes, Kutuzov thinks, it is necessary to have armies, because people expect nations to have them. But wise generals admit that armies should never fight. Indeed, Kutuzov cedes that he was forced to fight because everyone, in their foolishness, wants to have a battle: the soldiers, Napoleon, the tsar, the people. They have all worked themselves up to the expectation that a huge battle will take place, and therefore it will. But it is not the battle that defeats Napoleon, Tolstoy agues. What defeats Napoleon is the passive resistance of the whole Russian people, who are willing to give up their positions and houses and simply not participate. Napoleon entered Moscow, but it was nearly empty. No one greeted him as conqueror. Passive nonparticipation was as important to his defeat as any military action.

Bolkonsky's point is that if war were understood to be an unmitigated catastrophe, people would choose it less often.

What just war theories offer, sadly, is a mask behind which war goes on as it usually does. We can talk about noncombatant immunity, but as in the case of the Iraq War, between fifty and one hundred thousand have died as "collateral damage." This is arguably more than would have died under another popular insurrection against Saddam Hussein. In the thick of events, the limited and well-defined objectives have changed. And the means have arguably become less just.

Two hundred years ago, pioneers like Count Beccaria in Italy and John Howard in England visited prisons and publicized their findings to bring an end to the widespread use of judicial torture. We have in a single conflict rolled back much of the progress that has been made since that time, progress enshrined in the American Bill of Rights, the Geneva Conventions, and the findings of the Nuremberg trials, to name but three historical monuments to human progress that have now been at least partly discredited.

In a modified theory of pacifism, war would not be contemplated unless civilization itself were at risk. And when war was initiated, for deterrence effect it would be carried out in a way that was so brutal that people would think twice about trying the experience again. Or at least that seems to be what Bolkonsky proposes in his musings on the night before he is mortally injured.

But no amount of historical awareness of the brutality of war seems to deter it. In this respect, war differs little from other forms of justice or punishment. Routinely, civilized nations believe that shutting a person away for a large portion of his or her life, taking away earning power, taking away parenting, the support of children and family members, twisting their sexuality, disrupting a community—all that is directly and indirectly the consequence of imprisonment—amounts to a fair penalty. This kind of punishment, we say, is a useful deterrent for crimes such as taking a recreational drug or stealing a car.

But it doesn't work. Modified pacifism, temporized pacifism, is a sop to people whose feelings and sensibilities have been educated by cultures that believe in the efficacy of war. It is no more than that. Tolstoy recognizes that Bolkonsky, in addition to trying to frame a theory consistent with his growing faith, is also expressing self-disgust. How could things have come to such a place? Why is there no alternative? How weak and despicable are the human creatures who cannot find means to avoid such carnage. How weak and despicable is he who will in fact rise in the morning and stand by, waiting for an absurd almost accidental death. Tolstoy's answer to war, a few chapters later, is different and more pacifist. Napoleon may rule Moscow, but he rules nothing because the people will not obey or follow him. They would rather lose their property and subsist on minimal rations. And in the nothing Napoleon rules he is forced to see precisely the value of what he has accomplished. In the end, it is the massive and passive resistance of the Russian people that defeat the invader, not the armies.

Bolkonsky wrestles with an issue that C. S. Lewis and other critics of pacifism also pose. Somewhere there must be a threat of force behind the peaceful gestures. The force may be the threat of total war, as Bolkonsky mused, or it may be the very presence of large armies to serve as a deterrent, as Kutuzov reasons. It may be that among the most effective pacifists in the world are ordinary police officers in jurisdictions throughout the world, including those in places like England, where officers do not carry firearms. Much of their work involves precisely the capacity for understanding, the capacity for swallowing some measure of abuse that Jesus describes in the Beatitudes. Is there a modified pacifism that differs from Tolstoy's two proposals? Bolkonsky muses that if war were always a holocaust, we would not fight. Kutuzov recognizes that in the end it is the passive resistance of a population that matters, not the battles.

If one were to adopt a modified pacifism that allowed for some use of force, the question is then what level of force is sufficient to stand behind the methods of peace, for whatever we build and stockpile, we tend to use at one time or another, saving nuclear weapons (so far). During the Cold War, the Mutual Assured Destruction (MAD) policy, associated with Edward Teller, "father of the hydrogen bomb," was one way of framing the issue just as Bolkonsky did. MAD proposed to make nuclear war impossible by guaranteeing that the result would be the end of the world. Unfortunately MAD did not prevent the superpowers from carrying out a plethora of small and vicious proxy wars across Africa and Asia.

Return however to the picture of Napoleon in control of Moscow. Such a scenario is similar to the one the world faces in North Korea. There will be no uprising there, because it appears that the people do not know how miserable they are. They are told on their only radio channel that they are better off than the rest of the world, even though they are starving. Kim Jong II, unlike Napoleon, feels no frustration at ruling a place reduced to starvation, a place without an economy that can participate in the world. A military "solution" offers only the possibility of horrible losses in neighboring nations.

Only a pacifist solution holds any promise of success. As one columnist put it, the most powerful weapon the United States can use is to send fat business executives to do trade in North Korea. Their wealth and obesity would send the message that conditions are indeed different elsewhere. Knowledge and negotiation will make the difference, as they have in China. Similarly, the most impressive work for peace that Americans can do today is to address poverty, education, racism, and other problems in our own nation, so that it becomes a model for others. We are not in a strong position to export advice or assistance when our own house is so visibly in disorder.

One reason war continues to be attractive is what might be called the "illusion of successful empire" that has been part of the official world story. Works like the histories of Oswald Spengler, Arnold Toynbee, and even Edward Gibbon suggest that there have been major world powers that have controlled large parts of the globe through force of arms. The Pax Americana after World War II was to be like the Pax Romana, a kind of terrestrial peaceable kingdom, if one didn't look too closely. The colonial period that declined after the war conveyed a similar impression, and since Francis Fukuyama's declaration a few years ago of "the end of history," many political theorists believed that there might be not only a Pax Americana but even a reign of justice and world democracy in short order.

On closer inspection, however, such apparent miracles of order as the British Empire to its end in the 1960s, depended on conquest, rule by treaty, and other mechanisms. Hardly had Nigeria been organized, for example, and that partly under continued Muslim rule in the North, than the colonial era was over. And even a cursory study of an issue such as slavery indicates that there are probably as many if not more slaves now as in the past. Some live under modified conditions of servitude, even in the United States. For every small victory, such as the replacement of slave children as camel jockeys by robots in the Persian Gulf, there is a deeper story of continued slave trade. Force, in other words, offers only partial evidence that it has ever been successful. Under the myth that there have been successful empires created by force lies a less satisfactory reality, as the last few years of extravagant hopes for the quick establishment of liberal democracies in Afghanistan and Iraq have shown again.

The most to which a pacifist perspective could concede regarding force might be the concession that some form of international military unit might need to intervene in extreme situations. For example, Vietnam invaded Cambodia in 1978 to put an end to the genocide there. Perhaps, since international agencies seem unable to act, a group of smaller national armies *might* be justified.

But wait. Has not history shown arms to be more addictive and habit-forming than cocaine? Have we not created a situation in which it is more likely that the "nuclear club" will grow? That arms races will continue even in places where there is insufficient clean running water?

Others who argue for such a position have suggested that force would have prevented the outbreak of genocide in Rwanda in recent years. Perhaps. But what would such an approach have required? Enough troops to encircle the nation and patrol the cities? For how long?

In the case of the Falklands, would not serious economic sanctions against Argentina have had a strong chance of bringing about not only a return of the islands but also the demise of a dangerous government? Of course, Saddam Hussein proved immune to sanctions, as many looked the other way and permitted extensive illegal sale of oil and other commodities.

A modified form of pacifism might take two additional forms, however. One has a long history both of success and of being disregarded. Neutral nations continue to implement the policy. Perhaps the earliest formal statement of the view was made by Mo Tzu, a contemporary of Confucius, who in the face of political chaos in China proposed two ideas: First, pacifism is the morally and spiritually preferred position. Second, the way you maintain peace is to make an attack on you too costly. Therefore defensive arms are permitted. His teachings saved many small Chinese states.

A second reformulation of pacifism is consistent with del Vasto's position that in extreme cases of attack, even saints are likely to strike out instinctively. History shows that some important struggles have been brought to an end not by large battles between well-organized national armies but rather by guerilla war or local insurgencies. The Soviet experience in Afghanistan demonstrates the effectiveness of loosely organized local groups against a foreign invader.

Similarly, what effectiveness ought to be assigned to the French resistance and the Polish Home Army, which may have counted as many as a million members during World War II? Horrible as was the experience of those partisans, their form of war had perhaps the peculiar virtue of denying the combatants institutional faces. What they did was done in their own communities, with a constant awareness of the potential costs to themselves and to other community and family members. How different is such war, not merely psychologically but also morally, from the clinical and distant deterrent theory of Mutual Assured Destruction, with its large nuclear weapons, its missiles that strike from afar?

The evidence is mixed and the issues still murky. At best, perhaps one might justify wars when civilization was at risk and when the combatants were citizens, not institutionalized armies. Is a reformulated just war theory possible? Or is it an illusion?

6

Just War Reformulated

A reexamination of the criteria for just war, in the light of this body of evidence, leads to the following proposal for a revision of the theory.

Just Cause

The only conceivable just cause is a threat to the continuation of civilization, defined in such terms as the survival of the world's core of peoples and values. As support for this notion, consider the world's behavior not in the case of wars actually fought but in cases where the world decided that the justification was insufficient. These examples are complex, because they raise endless questions of geopolitics, race, religion, and economics.

The Dalai Lama has spent a lifetime advocating the cause of Tibet. Tibet has been both an independent nation and a part of China at various times in the past eight hundred years. Currently it is occupied by China. A case can certainly be made that the Chinese have carried out a campaign of suppression against the Tibetan culture and against its ruling Tibetan Buddhist hierarchy in particular. Monasteries have been destroyed, monks killed or imprisoned. Chinese nationals have been favored in the new economy. It may be that no one has gone to war to free Tibet because there is little chance of success; a war against China is not easy to contemplate. Another reason might be that in spite of the persecution, the Tibetan way of life and its religion are continuing. This is not a case of genocide against a people or a way of life. In fact, while the Dalai Lama has not returned to Tibet, other important Tibetan Buddhist leaders living in the West have made visits to their home nation. The leader of the Sakya tradition, for example, has made several trips home.

The problem of freedom for Tibet is further compounded by the nature of Tibet's form of government. In a sense, Tibet raises some of the same issues as Kuwait. The traditional Tibetan religious government, while picturesque, constituted one of the most oppressive forms of theocracy in world history. From a liberal western perspective, there is only a weak case that a Tibetan government would provide more justice than a Chinese communist one. The Dalai Lama was a divine monarch, the Panchen Lama a divine religious leader. They ruled with a kind of absolutism seldom seen elsewhere in the world. While it is true that the people of Tibet may prefer their own totalitarian culture to the one imposed by the current Chinese regime, from a western democratic perspective, neither government makes a satisfactory case that it provides sufficient freedom. Implicitly, the world chooses its causes, and when there is no genocidal threat, there is often little will to go to war.

It may be that the actual criterion in use by contemporary world powers is a threat to the existence of civilization as we know it. Sometimes, however, the threat itself is exaggerated (as perhaps in the case of relatively small terrorist attacks). And sometimes, world powers allow a lower threshold of threat to be convincing because they have no intent of going to war themselves. Rather, they wage a war in one or two small proxy states whose citizens more often than not belong to a different race or ethnic group. Hence Vietnamese, Cambodians, Iraqis, Afghanis, Iranians, Kurds, and others died in larger numbers than Russians or Americans in the proxy wars of Southeast Asia and the Near East.

From a radical Christian perspective, however, even such a revised criterion is faulty because it is not obvious that civilization as we know it is worth preserving in its entirety. The Baha'i philosophy makes an important point when it argues that many more prophets are to come who will bring additional visions to the world as the world is prepared to hear them. A Christian might respond that the additional prophecy has been received but not yet heard.

Contemporary moral and religious pluralism assigns high value to cultural diversity, democratic forms of government, and equality for women. Yet maintaining cultural diversity runs counter to the other two values, because many cultures are antidemocratic and misogynistic. Of course, the dominant cultures do not meet a very high religious standard for compassion, service to others, simplicity, humility, and other virtues.

Whatever system of values you embrace, it is hard to argue that the world as we know it is worth preserving in its entirety. Therefore maintaining business as usual is not a justifiable criterion for going to war unless one were convinced that even the limited virtues of existing civilization were likely to be replaced by utter barbarism.

Of course, even asking these questions assumes that the people who make decisions about war are acting rationally. Two centuries ago Jonathan Swift offered a devastating critique of the European wars of his time when he suggested in his *Tale of a Tub* that the choice to fight was always grounded in personal psychopathology. Many of the largest wars have been impelled by a need to find a quick solution to some social crisis. But pacifist approaches to conflicts provide the only long-term solutions to such emerging crises.

Limited Objective

There is no such thing as a limited objective. If a threat to civilization is the only justifying cause, obviously such a threat will not arise unless a substantial group of individuals with significant military power has created a culture determined to destroy civilization as we know it. Such a counter-civilization might be stopped in its tracks by arms, but it will not be transformed by arms, and therefore a full response must include a program of redevelopment and reeducation. Moreover, by the time such a genuine threat arises, the emergency is such that no limited approach is likely to succeed. If such a threat were to arise, it would be due to a massive failure of communication.

In practice, it would be very difficult to justify a war on even this ground, because the alliance on the side of "justice" would probably include many nations and peoples who did not fully share a "just" view of society. World War II had far from perfect justification on the grounds of this criterion. Germany and Japan were overthrown, and then extensive efforts were made to rebuild and acculturate the two nations, with great success. But Eastern Europe was sacrificed in the process. In retrospect, the war's objective was limited to recovering Germany and Japan, though it was not limited in the sense that years of investment were required. The original limited objective of defending various Eastern European nations was abandoned as too costly. And the alliance that won the war included nations with political and moral philosophies directly opposed to those of the chief European and American allies.

It seems that where the objective is truly small, it can be achieved by other means, but where it is large, the limits are likely to be very poorly defined and in no real sense limited at all, because they usually change quickly in response to emerging conditions. The criterion of limited means seems to fit well only such situations as, say, the recent Turkish occupation of an unpopulated Greek islet where, in the absence of sufficiently cordial relations, a show of force by navy cutters seems to be necessary to maintain borders.

Currently, international terrorism demonstrates why wars cannot have limited objectives. A war against terrorism at this time means a war against whatever historical and cultural forces drive tens of thousands of individuals from a religious group with nearly two billion members to strike against a rival culture. There are roughly 2.3 billion Christians and 1.8 billion Muslims; the two groups are spread over scores of nations. Worse still are the divisions within Islam that are now at war; the Shia and the Sunni have been at odds since the death of Muhammad. Since fear of the other is one of the chief drivers of the anger, any military response will necessarily aggravate the conditions that lead people to become terrorists. No solution is possible short of a new accommodation between cultures or complete occupation of the dozens of nations inhabited by a third of the world's population. Where the threat is large and deeply rooted in differences of culture and faith, military means cannot succeed and the objectives cannot be limited.

All of this assumes an additional reality that sadly cannot be assumed: that nations will tell the truth about their objectives. If oil and energy are reasons for a war, it does not necessarily follow that such reasons must be morally wrong. But if the issues are not placed on the table, the complexities and alternatives cannot be usefully discussed.

Just Ends

Just ends are impossible to define when any truly just end would require cultural transformation. A criterion that may have made some sense with respect to moving the borders of a European nation by a county one direction or another makes less sense where the issues are fully opposed views of existence. What would have happened if the United States in fighting Japan had made it clear early on that its objective was not merely to defeat the Japanese forces but also to establish a new form of government and culture that would be opposed to war? Open discussion of such a goal would have raised deep ethical and political questions, particularly in the context of the internment of American Japanese. Conversely, what would have been just about stating the goal as defeating the Japanese and leaving their nation in ruins? Superficially, from the perspective of criminal justice, one could argue that people who start a war need to be stopped and also punished, and therefore justice consists exactly in defeating them and then leaving them to starve and suffer. The world does not appear to be comfortable with that kind of definition for "just war." Yet the alternative smacks of cultural colonialism and is equally unsatisfactory and controversial.

However admirable was the Marshall Plan or the American occupation of Japan, those were not part of an initial war plan or of the immediate objectives of the war. A modified just war theory would need to add at least an eighth criterion to satisfy the present world: it will be possible to restore the defeated nation to autonomy, with its cultural identity intact, to the degree that such an identity can be reframed in pacifist terms. This is, after all, what was expected of Japan and Germany: that their future governments would be less warlike than the governments of those who conquered them. How curious that nations would prescribe pacifist tendencies to others but not adopt them themselves. It seems that one of the highest and most just ends of war, as defined by the practice of the last fifty years, is to create pacifist states or at least states whose view of war is in agreement with that old Chinese philosopher Mo Tzu.

Noncombatant Immunity

Noncombatant immunity is also an admirable goal in warfare, but impossible in practice, particularly where differences in race or language are present. In the wake of the Hundred Years War, perhaps it seemed possible to recommend that future armies carry out their battles in safe isolation from cities, like retired generals playing with squads of lead soldiers on a dining table. What would serve as a good practical example of a war that was carried out with real attention to sparing civilians? Even if one assumes that noncombatant immunity is not meant to apply to such groups as soldiers' family members, to workers, to industries, or to supplies of food, electricity, or water, even if one limits the issue to sparing the lives of people who live on or near contested areas, is noncombatant immunity possible? The criterion seems to be designed to prevent atrocities such as the slaughter of whole cities after a victory, the deaths of the wounded, or the choice to set battles in underpopulated areas.

Has there been a war carried out in sufficient isolation from urban areas? One might think of the defeat of Bonny Prince Charlie, which took place at a field far enough away from the main population centers of England and Scotland, except for the ugly fact that the Battle of Culloden, the last land battle in Great Britain, was followed by a horrific episode of genocide. The British army slaughtered men, women, and children throughout the surrounding area and later raided the Highlands. And would any of the battles of World War I meet the noncombatant immunity standard?

Moreover, it seems unlikely that any group at the point of defeat would hesitate to take cover among civilians or to carry out a guerilla war from civilian bases. Mass civilian slaughter and reprisals have not declined as a result of new kinds of weapons or increased media attention. What events in recent years prove that the world has improved in this regard? The massacres in former Yugoslavia? Or Chechnya? Or the starvation of Iraqi children through sanctions? Or the broad and self-forgiving understanding of collateral damage? A criterion that cannot be satisfied is not of much use either before the fact, during a war, or while post mortems proceed.

Just Means

Just means is a way of limiting the horror of weapons, though it is difficult from a distance to see the difference between, say, the use of poison gas in World War I (outlawed) and actions such as the fire bombing of Tokyo or Dresden (not outlawed) or the carpet bombing of retreating troops in the Iraq desert (allowed). The justice in this case appears to be partly an aesthetic value rather than an ethical one. *Just* denotes not cruel or unusual, not prone to producing painful and protracted death. Yet *just* also seems to denote not especially ugly or disgusting, though precisely why gas is worse than fragmentation bombs, Agent Orange, or napalm has perhaps never been discussed in public. Dying of a deep penetrating wound is surely as bad as dying of a condition that disfigures the body's surface tissue.

This criterion may offer some salve to the imaginations and consciences of those who are not on the battlefield or in the hospitals, but it cannot mean much else. In fact, it has more to do with winning votes by sugarcoating the consequences of war than with actually justifying it. And for that reason, it is not so much a justification as a potential rationalization. The criterion of just means does not help to determine whether this or that particular war is in fact justified. Rather, it implies that any lack of justice in a war may be palliated by a promise not to hurt people too much when they are killed. So "just means" is not a suitable criterion at all. It ought not to be part of any such theory. Within the last year this issue has become prominent again as U.S. forces admitted to using white phosphorus in the campaign to "pacify" Fallujah, Iraq. Robin Coupland's essays, listed in the bibliography, offer a surgeon's perspective on international attempts to define categories of weapons and to outlaw weapons.

Just means, though, has a second definition that is particularly relevant to the present, when so much attention is paid to what is called terrorism. While war according to the rules includes such niceties as a formal declaration (the United States faulted Japan for the sneaky surprise attack on Pearl Harbor), terror strikes without a formal announcement of an objective or an offer of negotiation. So terror is by definition surprise. Terror also aims to defeat by being unpredictable in its victims and recognizing no distinction between combatants and noncombatants. It is also a method by which totalitarianism operates, whether the totalitarianism exercised by slavers controlling slaves in the ante-bellum South or the totalitarianism of any regime that oppresses a large population through atrocities designed to cow whole peoples.

Terror is the most unjust of means because it is also least open to any form of discussion. The mask of the terrorist negates humanity, compromise, and understanding. Having said all that, is there a meaningful difference between the unexpected terror of an attack by a suicide bomber and a large distant state with extraordinary military resources inflicting "surgical" attacks to defend a no-fly zone or to "take out" selected "assets"? Is it any less terrorizing when such a state explains civilian casualties as "collateral damage" and suffers no consequences? Is there any moral difference between superpower aggression and the act of a suicide bomber when the keys to both are secrecy and surprise?

Limited Means

Limited means are admirable too, in a theoretical way, though the reality is that in order to save personnel, armies tend to use everything they have short of nuclear weapons. The entire just war framework seems designed for a situation in which there is a clear and limited problem, a failure of negotiation, and potential for two armed groups to fight at a distance from anyone else. The Mexican-American war might serve as an example, because most of the combat took place where few people lived, and then vast amounts of territory were rather clinically transferred from one authority to another.

To limit means, a force needs to work itself up to kill and then coolly decide how thorough the killing will be. Is this really plausible? Most victors prefer not only to win but also to make a point—to do sufficient damage that the loser will be thoroughly humbled and unlikely to go to war again. In fact, victors will offer a pacific reason for smashing more than is purely necessary, because that little additional violence may serve to prevent the need for another war for a longer period. Here, in other words, the just war theory works against itself. In our often twisted and very human way of thinking, enough is never really enough, because it is always unclear how much *more* will guarantee that the message is conveyed.

Just war theorists have raised this issue repeatedly in the case of the two wars against Iraq. Wasn't it true that the first George Bush's decision to limit his war to restoring Kuwait and damaging the Iraqi army set the stage for the second war? Wouldn't *more* have been better?

Limited means is also a way of stating the importance of noncombatant immunity. If a force can be defeated without destroying the public infrastructure of roads, bridges, water, sewage, electricity, and medical care, so much the better. As in the case of "just means," "limited means" is not so much a criterion for justifying going to war as it is a criterion for justly prosecuting a war. In other words, it offers a platform for rationalizing a war once one has started, but it is not a very good trigger criterion for making the choice. The exception, of course, is if it were to be clear that a war could not be "won" unless one were to obliterate a nation with nuclear weapons and that was the only way to ensure a "reasonable chance of success."

The American experience in Vietnam offers a curious window into how discussions of just war might actually play out in history. It has been said that John Foster Dulles argued in favor of the use of nuclear weapons against Hanoi as the only sure way to "win" the war in its early stages. Senator Wayne Morse of Oregon traveled the United States during the later stages of the Vietnam War making a related point.

American studies after the Korean War demonstrated that the United States could not win a land war in Asia. In spite of these findings, America went to war anyway—just as America waged the second Iraq War without a rational plan for victory, nation building, or a clean exit. What is the use of a theory that is not invoked in such clear cases?

A Reasonable Chance of Success

In view of the difficulty of defining reasonable objectives, the most that war itself can promise (leaving aside the development efforts that are often promised as part of the war "package") is a temporary limitation of conflict and a postponement of further conflict. Some wars meet this criterion; other wars are attended with hardly any chance of success at all. World War II of course serves as the counter-example, and that example works well so long as one does not ask how the groundwork for that war was set in the punitive policies of the Treaty of Versailles. That treaty violated the unstated just-war criterion proposed here: that defeated states must be restored to viability and that the restoration must respect the culture.

Redefined in this way it is hard to imagine a circumstance that would constitute a just war, short of the world allowing some enormous threat to its very existence to arise over a period of a decade or more. Wars of the last few decades have often been framed in terms of threats to the survival of "our way of life," with pressure exerted on smaller nations to carry out the actual fighting, so that it was abundantly clear that the larger powers had little interest in any form of struggle to the death, aside from a struggle of rhetoric. What those wars have tended to demonstrate, in the end, has been the relative strength and independence of the nations that were at first seduced into participating. The Soviets never conquered Afghanistan; the United States supported Iraq's efforts against Iran but never made a significant impact on the political culture of Iraq itself.

Most recent wars never met what might be proposed as a second additional criterion for the old theory: a high level of international agreement that force is likely to help. Those who favor wars have attacked the pusillanimity, feckless-ness, or indecision of the United Nations. If even NATO al-lies will not support an effort, perhaps attention should be paid. Oddly, a threat to the continued existence of civiliza-tion as we know it may be emerging, in the form of global warming. Would it be logical, in terms of just war theory, for all the nations that have low energy consumption to go to war against the larger nations to stop them from heating up the earth?

Under what conditions, then, has just war theory ever been of much value? During the Islamic assault on Christian Europe perhaps? Or to justify local resistance to Western colonial assaults against the lands and cultures of two thirds of the world? By what standard were any of those wars a success in the long term? Just war theory's key weakness is that at present it can apply only to those nations that are likely to have the power necessary to pursue a war to success, and in the last century, few powers or alliances of powers have been able to assemble that much force.

It is hard, for example, to imagine contemporary France, Belgium, or Botswana engaging in a just war if success would be a criterion for making an assault. This comment is not intended to insult any smaller nation. A nation can be successful and praiseworthy without having a huge army and a capacity to throw nuclear weapons across the seas. The point is that all the talk of just war, in the present world political and military contexts, makes sense only when one speaks of less than a handful of nations that have large military establishments. Even then, the chance of success is unlikely, because the historic enemies of those same nations also maintain large armies, to the detriment of their mutual economic progress. India and Pakistan serve as an example. If you are a small nation, you can never meet the criterion of success; if you are a nation large or small with a huge military investment, you also cannot meet the criterion for success because your natural enemy has taken the advice of Mo Tzu and prepared a defense that would ruin you.

A handful of nations in the world maintain enormous armies at ruinous expense because they are locked in long-standing conflicts: India and Pakistan, the two Koreas, China and Taiwan, Iran and Israel. Two nations used to maintain large armies because they represented a larger competition: the United States and the Soviet Union. In spite of the fact that both possessed enough extra strength and financial resources to be able to protect home territory *and* carry out a war elsewhere, neither of those nations was or is able to carry out an invasion of a smaller power with success. Vietnam,

Afghanistan, and Iraq, among others, demonstrate that, even now, with all the technology that has been developed since the heyday of colonialism in the nineteenth century, a foreign occupying army cannot control another nation unless the occupier is willing to use all of its resources, drain itself of troops, and perhaps take away its ability to protect itself against another threat. Is the United States prepared to endure a draft, energy rationing, and other austerities to achieve a victory in the Middle East?

Does the concept of a superpower make any sense in such a world? Does the evidence suggest that a superpower has any special ability to provide stability or to "police the world," to use a cliché? Or does contemporary history rather show the inanity of any nation maintaining more than a small force that in extraordinary emergencies might be combined in an alliance to tackle some unimagined threat? It seems that Mo Tzu had a great deal of wisdom after all. Perhaps small defensive forces are justifiable for internal policing and to discourage external threats.

Last Resort

Armies in many states are simply used to support unjust regimes, which is one reason Costa Rica made the unusual choice to eliminate its army altogether and risk the unlikely possibility that some Central American neighbor might launch a war of conquest. Nations of that size have little hope should a superpower choose to intervene, as the United States has done repeatedly in Panama. Conversely, most nations that have great rather than merely sufficient power have maintained that power in order to carry out a war of conquest. Nations that plan for conquest violate by definition the criterion of last resort. Such nations are so clearly intent on waging war precipitously that their trigger for "last resort" is far too easily pressed. Such nations suffer from a lack of imagination as to what might be done by other means to address the problems of their own citizens and the issues facing others on this planet.

So there cannot be a just war if the theory stands either unrevised or revised as proposed. The best that can be said is that under cataclysmic circumstances, people who maintained defensive capabilities and police powers might be induced to sacrifice themselves in combat to ensure survival of their most fundamental tenets of faith and culture. A revised just war theory would need to include at least two additional criteria. There must be international agreement that a war is worth waging. And there must be a demonstrated capacity to restore the conquered territories, with full respect for their cultures.

What is the alternative? Unjust wars of various shades of darkness, and dirty wars. What is also left is the recognition that pacifism proposes the first question that must be answered: Just what are those values that are worth preserving in this world? If we were to define the last resort, the most basic human values worth defending at any cost, what would those be? And why are we not spending more time building those values?

7

Peaceful Action

A just estimate of the worth of a pacifist philosophy must begin with the understanding that pacifism is far more than merely a refusal to use weapons or a distaste for the horrors of war. And there is no point in pretending that many of us have a genuine distaste for war, since our literature and our entertainments—from the *Iliad* forward to the latest video games—prove the contrary. We are bloodthirsty, lured by fast solutions to problems, eager to put on the mask of temporary immortality and put aside whatever ethics we have in an imaginary pursuit of victims.

Most new video games come with the immortality option. No matter how many bullets you take into your torso, you can keep on killing for as long as you want. You can be Shiva, destroyer of worlds, and Kali, who vomits blood and wears a necklace of skulls. Of the world's major early epics, it is one from the Arab world, *Gilgamesh*, that breaks out of the normal epic mold and offers a story of deep friendship and a desire to overcome death. The *Iliad* merely expresses disgust with the addiction to force, especially if one reads it as did Simone Weil. The *Bhagavad-Gita* tells a story of a leader who recoils against war, only to be persuaded by God himself that war is right.

Our play may or may not have sublimated our violence in the past, but increasingly our play is as violent as war. We acculturate ourselves to still more violence as nightly entertainment, and we know too that our entertainments are spilling over into our lives. Pacifism therefore requires a re-orientation of how we must spend our time. And as leisure time grows in the developed world, this challenge becomes more pressing.

What then is pacifism? It must begin with the understanding that the civilization in which we live is at some important level not worth saving. Our civilization has evolved or has been designed to produce the inequities and suffering that surround us. The answer to the problem of human evil is that we have made it.

When at the end of *Candide*, Voltaire's character says, "*Il faut cultiver notre jardin*" (we must cultivate our own garden), he states his conclusion that while we may not be able to fix all the evil, the problem is nevertheless our responsibility. In fact, we have an ethical imperative to try to repair at least the small corner where we live. It is necessary to cultivate our garden, and our garden most broadly construed is the world.

Why God allows evil or what theological justifications can be offered for evil or whether one believes or disbelieves in any religion because of evil are entirely beside the point. Those are diversions, as Pascal would have us understand diversion. They are games we play to avoid thinking about our existential situation. They are ways of passing the buck, pointing the finger, slipping away from the blame.

Defining Pacifism

Pacifism on further definition embodies the following characteristics and beliefs: First, any useful strategy for bringing an end to conflict will take a long time, because there exist no significant conflicts that do not have deep cultural histories and that do not involve meaningful differences in values. Peacemakers must get used to the idea that they are not likely to see the fruits of their efforts. But to be unable to see a vineyard mature is no reason to plant no shoots.

It follows that pacifists should not be passive. They should not limit themselves to withdrawing from conflicts, to refusing to bear arms, or to living apart from the rest of the world. Individual believers may have other cogent reasons for withdrawal, of course. No disrespect toward any other pacifist position is intended here, because the last disadvantage pacifism needs is conflict among pacifists. That was one of the tragedies of pacifism during the Reformation period—that believers debated among themselves rather than presenting their ideas to others in ways that might be persuasive.

The Gospels address this issue of action in an oblique but nevertheless interesting way. In Matthew the Beatitudes are followed by a collection of sayings, including some very powerful words about the danger of adultery or having unseemly thoughts. Later Jesus says that if violence is wrong, so are angry words, which are sufficient themselves to land a sinner in a very bad place. Those verses make a single point: Don't wait for trouble to develop. At the first sign of danger, do something, intervene, control yourself. By extension, the passages suggest that wherever a moral danger is visible, it should be confronted. Moral people of any persuasion ought to be vigilant and quick to address seeds of disorder before they can develop into threats that break the community. Solutions take a long time because people take a long time to change, and therefore it is everyone's duty to act early and continuously.

Pacifism demands a high standard of personal morality, humility, simple living, and a conscious effort to speak only from what one knows to be true. Martin Luther King's four steps for a nonviolent campaign emphasize finding out the facts, if the truth can indeed be discovered, and then working to purify one's motives and confront one's biases.

Characteristics of the Pacifist

Without much information, there are few solutions that one can bring to any crisis. What the Beatitudes recommend instead is a set of attitudes and expectations that may open the way to solutions in the face of conflict. First is deep sorrow at the state of things and therefore a profound sense of dissatisfaction. Second, peacemakers are then cautioned that any light cast into the shadows will stimulate howls of protest. Even asking questions, since that is all a truly humble person can do without guessing at the answers, will produce criticism and disregard. Third, one is to approach conflict with a deep hunger for justice but without preconceptions about what justice may be. Sorrow, openness to ideas and facts, hunger—these attitudes and feelings fit someone who has been utterly defeated, someone who has come to the end of every resource and who desires nothing but positive change.

When Lanza del Vasto in 1957 wrote to the French nation about the use of torture in the campaign against Algerian independence fighters, torture whose consequences and stories still percolate into the French press, torture that is still leading to confessions late in life from military officers and to trials and continued public anguish, he simply said that the situation had taken away his desire to eat. Therefore he would choose to fast publicly to draw attention to the emerging crisis. Even if he had been able to propose a clear solution to the challenges of the Algerian civil war, he might not have done so, because solutions take away the need for other people to engage themselves in the issues. A pacifist is therefore reluctant to suggest immediate steps that can be taken. Merely stopping a bad behavior, however beneficial it may be, will not induce others to consider what was wrong and to change their own perspectives and values.

A pacifist is required to ask obvious questions and to use the nonviolent method of speech and inquiry to probe social and personal disorder. Questions will lead to discomfort and reaction. Those who ask questions will be treated as Jesus predicted, with censure, calumny, and spite. So a pacifist must understand that he or she will be an irritant, and that criticism is a sign that the questions are at least being heard at that superficial level where they provoke denial.

Peter Kropotkin's critique of pacifists makes a point here. Pacifists create conflict by protesting, he observed, and those campaigns lead others to react with violence. So pacifists are people who provoke violence. Therefore pacifists are little different from other revolutionaries who initiate social change with bombs. Martin Luther King's response to this type of reasoning was to point out that one doesn't really have a choice about being labeled an extremist. Jesus was an extremist for love who rose above the norm; others are extremists for hate who fall beneath the norm. King was willing to recognize that in some sense members of the Ku Klux Klan were useful because at least they were engaged with the issues, unlike the majority of the population, who merely acquiesced in the state of things. Could it be that, as King suggested, the Klan actually helped the civil rights cause?

In the face of opposition, the pacifist must then be prepared to make sacrifices, up to and including the sacrifice of life itself. In this respect, the pacifist differs not at all from those who choose the way of violence. Historically, pacifists have accepted death with as much courage as any soldier. C. S. Lewis, who must have been strongly attracted to pacifism to attack it so fiercely, remarked that no nation builds monuments to those who "run away." But, in fact, nations do honor the practitioners of pacifism and nonviolence for their peacemaking and their creativity.

Finally, peacemakers must accept failure as an outcome, at least if the outcome is measured in terms of a single lifetime. If it takes a generation for personal and social change to allow people in the United States to face old injustices related to the labor movement, the Civil Rights Movement, or the internment of Japanese Americans, then any worker for peace must expect that deep change will take a generation at a minimum. To live with an expectation of failure is to share an experience with those who use violence as a tool, because violence so often breaks out anew from the embers and ashes left from previous wars.

Do the Gospels speak about longer-range hopes? Certainly they do with respect to the lives of individuals. What may be less clear is the extent to which the wisdom of the Gospels serves as a guide for the world's most pressing need: The meek shall inherit the earth. But what are the peacemakers to do in the meantime? What kind of organized witnessing, what kinds of organized hoping are possible so that communities together can imagine an alternative world? Can communities imagine what steps might be taken to realize objectives that may lie two to six generations in the future?

The Holy Grail

One of the world's most powerful legends can be interpreted as a deeply pacifist story. I referred earlier to the search for the Holy Grail as a literary motif, one that emerged sometime in the twelfth century. Some read the story as a celebration of knighthood and therefore a glorification of military virtues. Others find in the story what they believe or speculate to be a secret narrative about the travels of Jesus of Nazareth and the location of his possible descendants.

Others read the story as a metaphor for the spiritual search that leads to direct experience of God.

The grail knight in every version sets off as a soldier, heavily armed but at the same time inspired with a desire to become spiritually perfect. The knight understands imperfectly that this quest is different from other quests. He carries a sword, but he knows that moral conduct and prayer are as important on the quest as any of his more familiar tools: his armor, his steed, his lance, and his shield. In some of the poems, the shield is described in spiritual terms to point out that the physical armor is merely a metaphor for spiritual virtues that will help the knight to achieve the quest.

The knight fights several battles, barely winning some, and finds himself occasionally humiliated in battle. Oddly, and quite contrary to any military mission he has ever joined, he travels alone, so that the size of his military force is irrelevant. Still stranger, he has no geographical objective and no map. He is on "the quest." He is out to fight the world if necessary, but he has no particular foe to overcome. He would like to meet God or find the grail or do good, whatever the quest is destined to bring. That is all.

To put this in terms of the familiar just war theory, the grail knight has no just cause to fight, because his aim is spiritual knowledge, which cannot be won by fighting or killing anything. The means he carries with him, his armament, is out of proportion to his objective and utterly inappropriate for the task, which is to find truth and peace. His objective is undefined, because he knows neither what this peace is nor where it can be located. In fact, his combats bring him nothing but grief, while his incidental behavior, his prayer, and his treatment of others are what lead him toward his goal. He has no hope of success as a warrior, because he cannot compel God to reveal himself or to give him what he seeks. Moreover, his objective is not limited, because it embraces a desire for knowledge of the ultimate. He helps various noncombatants, and perhaps that is one reason he may be blessed and succeed.

In another sense, no one he actually fights has much to do with his objective. Rather, they are people he happens to meet along the way who want to pick fights with him. His opponents, in other words, are like the kinds of after-the-fact justifications that military leaders cite when they have a murky idea for going to war and then declare that their real reasons are identical to whatever enemies appear by chance during the course of thrashing around, invading, and occupying. His destination is obscure, because in fact what the legend teaches is that the true battle, like the true quest, is everywhere and present at all times. War never ought to be a response to some emergent crisis. Evil is a permanent state of affairs that can be found in all directions. Therefore it is foolish to think that justice will be found by waiting for a particularly egregious instance of evil and then applying a complex set of just-war criteria to decide what, if any, action should be taken. Moreover, the most useful weapons turn out to be those of the spirit and the intellect.

What an odd figure this grail knight seems to be. He pursues a mission with all the wrong tools, looking as silly as a doctor who might arrive in an operating theater with a cosmetics kit or a set of pruning shears. He thinks he is going to a war that will bring some kind of ultimate peace, but in fact nothing he does meets any standards for a just war, and he does not yet understand the kind of peace he wants to find. Nor does he understand that the only good he is likely to do will be done as a peacemaker rather than as a warrior. The grail legend undercuts the whole warrior myth out of which it springs.

Meanwhile, a real challenge awaits him. If he is fortunate, one day he will meet an opportunity in the form of a castle that appears out of nowhere. He doesn't realize that the castle has been there all along, and that the whole process of wandering has had no purpose except to offer him a chance for a moral education. The castle is here and now, everyplace and at every time, just as the grail is everywhere at all times, ready to be found if one asks the right questions and looks for it with the right intent.

The castle looks formidable and well fortified, but in fact the doors are wide open and everyone inside is welcoming. At first, most of the residents are interested in meeting a new person who just might be able to help out, particularly if the newcomer can help without causing too much embarrassment or making change too painful. Everyone knows that something is dreadfully wrong not only in the castle but also in the whole land. The king is sick; the harvests have failed. All the conditions exist as described in that oldest of prayers, the Shema, in which God promises the people of Israel to be in relationship with them if they observe the law but threatens a failure of rain and good crops if they have fallen away into disobedience.

The good and potentially successful knight then displays a set of familiar behaviors. He has good manners. He is gentle. He sorrows for the sickness he sees about him. He prays and tries to follow God's will as he sets aside his armor and dons a simpler set of garments. He washes himself both physically and ritually. He sits at the feast to which he is invited and listens carefully while watching a drama reveal itself in the awkward behavior of his hosts. He is offered several opportunities to interact. Depending on the version of the tale, he may ask the meaning of the procession that takes place during dinner. Or he may ask who is served the feast in a secret room. Or he may have an opportunity simply to ask why the kingdom has come to its present condition.

The knight then faces his greatest temptation. War has

this in its favor: it focuses human attention on an objective. If one of the blessings of human consciousness is that kind of "flow" described by Mihaly Csikszentmihaly, the contemporary psychologist, one might speculate that the "high" experienced in times of crisis derives from possessing a strong motivation to stay focused on a goal that is shared by many others. People who in the ordinary run of events seek out diversions to waste free hours or find themselves incapable of concentrating on difficult tasks suddenly discover new capacities for single-minded application.

The grail knight has maintained battle readiness for months and has found many enemies to defeat. Once in the castle, however, he is at ease and surrounded by that choice of diversions that historically have been categorized as the "three temptations": the lust of the senses, the lust for possessions (or "more"), and the lust for status or for continued existence itself. Military recruiting advertisements play on this reality. The potential recruit, who is lost without a career, struggling in school, and awash in bad choices, is offered focus, a sense of mission, and training for a successful career. No other vocation, our folk culture tells us, is better for helping drifters to shape up. Confused and troubled kids are often told to join the army to find themselves and get the discipline necessary to make it.

The Beatitudes offer an alternative in hunger. Jesus recommends that we stay hungry for righteousness, that we cultivate the ability to focus our efforts specifically by developing a powerful sense of grief for the suffering around us while we hunger for solutions. No doubt physical hunger is also an aid to concentration, as it has been in the cases of many pacifist or nonviolent leaders in the last century, such as Mohandas Gandhi, Lanza del Vasto, and Cesar Chavez. Pacifist wisdom offers an alternative to war's ability to focus human effort.

Our knight, meanwhile, finds himself surrounded by the temptations of dinner and conversation at precisely the moment when he must make the most critical choice in his life. If he asks the question, he achieves the quest, which is to bring light to a dark place and to begin change by pointing out the obvious. He will then have done God's will and in a sense have seen God. In more extreme versions, he literally sees the grail, the cup Christ used at the Last Supper, and therefore he sees the true blood of God and dies to this world. Those who achieve the quest in any case are likely to die, because the transformation they start is likely to consume them or because those who face change may kill the knight. If, on the other hand, the knight fails to seize his opportunity, he finds himself escorted silently to the door the next morning, and as soon as he turns his back on the castle of opportunity, it disappears, only to reappear the next time someone comes who may have the courage to ask the right question.

Either way, the outcome is a kind of failure, as the world measures success. Victory leads to a kind of annihilation in death or effort, a victory that may leave no historical record. Failure leads to expulsion, excommunication, disregard, and a sense of humiliation. Either way, the outcome is a success, because the quest is achieved and a people have a chance to be healed or because the knight survives the humiliation and may succeed next time if he draws the proper lesson from his experience. Either way, the knight also has an opportunity to realize that the truly transforming work was not done by the sword. Instead, the real work encompassed spiritual preparation and intellectual effort, accompanied by empathy and personal emptiness. The real work is also merciful.

Therefore, the grail legend, which comes out of the great military and Christian literature of the West, embodies a surprise. It is a story about pulling away the mask of militancy, behind which the knight hides, the mask that carries his pride and his reputation, because when the real test comes, it is not a test of arms at all. There is no traditional enemy who can be attacked and defeated. Rather, the quest becomes a test of mind and spirit that he must pass alone and dressed in ordinary clothes. If anything, the elaborate rules of chivalry that he normally observes make it easier for him to continue to wear a mask, so that his most difficult task is to be a simple individual and to see past the layers of status that he has learned to attribute to himself and others. He must stop asking himself who that man at the end of the table is who looks like a good swordsman or what is the meaning of that star worn by another guest or who ranks first at the table or other questions about masks rather than reality. The reality is that this place is deeply sick and deeply in need of healing, deeply in need of someone who can sorrow and who can ask for consolation.

The story of the ultimate warrior turns out to be the story of the one who must put away his weapons entirely in order to make a difference and to achieve what he seeks, a personal knowledge of God and of himself. The quest must also be finished by the community, because the enemy is a community illness that all must choose to heal. Moreover, the grail castle is everywhere. The challenge is not something that will arise later or in a strange land. It is first of all in ourselves and in the way that the communities we have built deviate from the vision of the Beatitudes.

There is a curious sense in which one can see the grail story played out in the lives of senior statespersons in the world. Former President Jimmy Carter offers an example. After the mixed record of his administration, including the disastrous attempt to liberate the hostages at the American embassy in Tehran, he has spent the balance of his career doing the quieter and often more effective work of peace. Even figures such as Henry Kissinger, the Nixon-era hawk of the Vietnam War, have mellowed to some degree. Once they are out of the crucible of government, where the weapons of war come ready to hand and there are few voices to recommend solutions that will take longer than one presidential term to complete, leaders have the leisure to consider what might actually produce good results in the long term. This is not merely a matter of hindsight being twenty-twenty, but rather a reflection of how our political systems try to make significant social and political changes in relatively short periods of time, such as the length of a single presidential administration.

The system is therefore bent toward violence, because not to act looks like passivity, and only violent solutions can be implemented quickly. "More" tempts us to see resolution in devices that are big or many or fast or expensive. Pacifist answers require more personal change. When the grail knight asks what is wrong, the people in the sick nation must be prepared to change the way they live, in the same way that some of the solutions to contemporary wars might require sacrifices such as less use of energy resources and all that implies for the way people in the developed world carry on their lives. Pacifism requires that systems of government be capable of dreams and plans that take at least a generation to realize.

Jesus' encounter with the men intent on stoning an adulterous woman fits another aspect of the grail story well. They are warriors, those righteous men who encircle the woman with sharp stones in their trembling hands. They have found the evil in their community, and according to their law they are proceeding to carry out a just execution. As Wilfred Thesiger wrote about getting to know the Marsh Arabs, "You can usually get on terms with people by helping them to kill something." The justly angry crowd will form a bond of blood by mobbing together, stones in hand, to do the work of justice.

Beneath the dialogue as it has been passed down to us, there is a second conversation. Jesus' comment to the men amounts to a simple question: "What is going on here?" Their implicit answer is, "We are busy killing ourselves. We've found one of our number who does the same things we do, but she has sinned openly enough that we can make her a victim to our law and feel righteous about it." Jesus' reply merely points out a simple truth: They are engaged in self-slaughter, community slaughter. If justice means establishing a better community, then the violence they do today creates no justice. If they continue to lie to themselves about their own conduct, if they continue to wear the masks of city fathers, they will go on to find new victims and perpetuate the system of abuse and murder.

So the men drop their stones and walk away grumbling, having cut the critic off from community. They don't want to stay to talk about what they have learned. The peacemaker has paid a small but predictable price of exclusion, knowing that later he may be cursed. For all we know, the woman too will say a bad word for him, because she may face death another day. In any case, she has nowhere safe to lay her head. She too faces expulsion.

Is such a pacifism practical? What the grail legend teaches, as do the Beatitudes and many parables, is that we must ask the right questions, listen carefully for useful information, and decline to be sidetracked by the masks.

Still, the question remains: where is the peacemaker to start? What is the first step?

Study War No More
A short time ago someone held a dinner party with a

visiting Irish Protestant pastor who had come to America to demonstrate his gift as a flower arranger. Conversation coursed from flowers to other plant materials that are crafted into competitive arrangements. Before the dinner, the party walked together through a forest and scavenged interesting bits of bark, ferns, moss, and otherwise unusual living stuff that could be posed in vases. At dinner itself, the pastor was asked about awards he had won from British royalty in various contests of flower arrangers. Later and awkwardly, someone asked about the state of life in Northern Ireland, where the pastor led a church, and he spoke hesitatingly about conditions. A few people shared stories of war conditions, visits to Ulster, recollections of the historical events that were celebrated each year by the opposing parties, and stories about weapons and bombs.

Finally, someone asked the visitor outright where he stood in relation to the events of his country. Only then he revealed shyly that indeed he was an active peace leader. He brought parties from both sides together for conversation. He sponsored meetings of youth from both sides so that the hatreds of the past generations would be less likely to continue into the future. And then he spoke about his sacrifice, the times he had been abused and threatened, and how his own child had been captured, tortured, but finally released once his captors realized that he was the child of a peacemaker they respected, although they themselves were not ready to turn to peace.

One evening treated us to the masks, the images of the Queen conferring honors, the delightful flower shows, and the pastor's hobby. That same evening gave us also a predictable dialogue about war, with the covert delight that people take in stories of danger and accounts of weapons and hardware. The evening also gave us a completely alternative vision of life, in which the topic was neither the mask nor the pleasures of studying war, but rather the work of peace, the humility and self-effacement of the peacemaker, the sacrifices of the family, and the continuing resolve to work still in the face of pain and what sometimes looked like failure, though it was impossible yet to know the positive effects of his work on generations to come.

The third phase of the conversation, in which we entered his real world of suffering and peacemaking, felt indeed like entering a new cosmos. While it did not devalue the rest of the evening, it brought us face to face with a work that was self-evidently more important and that touched the lives of those present more deeply. We were, in the words of the old African-American spiritual, studying war no more. We had started the work, quite unexpectedly, of studying peace. Given a choice of two pictures, we had turned away from the familiar one, the one to which we were acculturated by the media, the one that was the focus of so much of our political dialogue, and we had looked instead at another world. The same world, of course, but one viewed in a different way, a way so different that all sense of what was right and wrong, significant and insignificant, capable of making an impact, capable of producing improvements—all of that was changed by the presence of an alternative vision that directed us to look at our world anew.

The first step in pacifism is merely to look at the world in a new way. To study war no more, but to study peace, to notice the extraordinary effectiveness of peaceful behavior in most of the world most of the time and to ask then the simple question, Why isn't that working here—wherever there is strife? Pacifism is practical in the end because it is the only approach to violence that can succeed in the long run.

Just war theory suffers from many contradictions. Most wars can be to some degree justified on both sides by using the constructs offered by the theory. Moreover, it is not clear that the theory functions as a public instrument for making wise choices. The best that can be said for military preparation is that small police or military powers, with the addition of appropriate international vigilance to prevent the rise of malignantly large forces, are probably sufficient to maintain a generally peaceful world. Larger armies increase the threat to the world, and in recent times, even very large states have not been able to use arms effectively to secure victories in battles against small states or to prevent civil wars and genocide.

Besides, it is increasingly clear that no one on this earth has an army large enough to address even a handful of the world's present conflicts. Yes, there may be fewer wars now than a generation ago, but they are intractable ones. We have made automatic weapons, land mines, rocket-propelled grenades, and other powerful tools of violence so readily available that there will never again be conflicts among unevenly armed opponents, as there were in the nineteenth century or as there were even in the first months of World War II. How many troops—and from what sinless nation—would it take to separate the factions of Darfur, the Hutu and Tutsi of Rwanda, the Shia and the Sunni, to offer only a fraction of the current list?

Some contemporary theorists ask what might be done quickly to help the innocent in such places as Rwanda and Darfur. Of course none of us is innocent where ethnic conflict is concerned. Nor is it clear that peacekeeping forces as we now use them can do more than postpone a continuation of civil war or ethnic conflict. Donations of food and teams of outside medical experts and negotiators can also help, but seldom for the long term. For reasons such as these, Pope John Paul II concluded that military intervention in such crises was not acceptable, though humanitarian assistance was to be encouraged. We may need a fresh start at deliberation that grows out of a mutual hunger not to do things the way we have done them so far. Like the grail knight, we may need to begin with open eyes and a readiness to see the burned-out and sick lands in which we live. We need to ask what is going on and to wait in hunger rather than rush to an answer.

War carries a high cost, and the apparent successes of war are often followed by disappointment. Mo Tzu's ancient teaching about defensive preparation could be a useful guide, and as a matter of fact, most nations appear to follow precisely his kind of advice. Arm lightly, avoid wars, and form strong alliances in case of emergency. If you must arm, maintain a citizen service that does not lead to a special soldier class socialized into wearing masks and living double lives with different ethics and compartmentalized identities. And yet to make even this concession to the promise of war means that one is prepared to think in terms of immediate solutions, fast solutions, false solutions rather than in terms of long-term commitments to a different way to live. Violence teaches that violence is an acceptable solution. Violence always advertises itself as the only solution. So once violence goes away, those who have lived under its shadow can think of no other measures to take except a renewal of violence.

Only pacifism is fully consistent with the central teachings of the Christian faith. Pacifism requires constant activism, because at its best it is not a response to emerging crises but rather a program of creating an alternative civilization that will not suffer from the misunderstandings, injustice, and unequal distribution of resources that bring about war. Pacifism is the only approach to conflict that has promise to address underlying cultural differences, because pacifism at its core aims to bring people together in humility to discuss their deepest needs.

A pacifist way, however, requires peoples to think beyond the limits of their own lifetimes and to recognize that most truly difficult human conflicts are grounded in longstanding cultural differences that will take at least several generations to heal. A pacifist way of action requires us to recognize that the conflict begins in our own persons, because we have been acculturated to wanting "more." We want fast solutions. We have developed a taste for violence. And we have become too passive in the face of questions that cry out to be asked. Pacifism cannot be a response; it must be a way of living.

For these reasons, while a reformulation of just war theory is possible, and while peacemaking principles have been advanced as an alternative to just war theory, it may be time now to pause before implementing any form of intervention, however well meaning. Our first task is to set our own houses in order, so that people with competing views of life will look to us with admiration rather than with fear, disgust, and anger. In the words of the Gospels, we are in a poor place to suggest how to remove the speck in a neighbor's eye when we have a log in our own (Matthew 7:5).

At the heart of the "manual" lie the strange Beatitudes, and they point the way to a pacifist and utterly transforming vision of civilization. It begins with hunger, the initial step toward emptiness.

Bibliography

Anonymous. *Agenbyte of Inwit*. Oxford: Early English Text Society, 1922.

———. *Sir Gawain and the Greene Knight*. London: Dent, 1963.

Arendt, Hannah. *The Human Condition*. Chicago: University of Chicago Press, 1958.

Aristotle, ed. by W. D. Ross. "Nichomachean Ethics" in *Aristotle Selections*. New York: Scribner's, 1938.

Auden, W. H. "September 1, 1939," *Collected Poems*. New York: Random House, 1940.

Beccaria, Cesare. *On Crimes and Punishments*, translated by Henry Paolucci. New York: Macmillan, 1963.

Bhagavad-Gita. Gorakhpur: Gita Press, 1966.

Blunden, Edmund. *Undertones of War*. London: Penguin, 1937.

Boulding, Elise. *The Underside of History: A View of Women Through Time*. Newberry Park, Calif.: Sage, 1992.

Butler, Joseph. *Fifteen Sermons*. London: SPCK, 1970.

Chan, Wing-Tsit. *A Source Book in Chinese Philosophy*. Princeton, N.J.: Princeton, University Press, 1963.

Coupland, Robert M. "Abhorrent Weapons and 'superfluous Injury or unnecessary suffering': from field surgery to law." http://bmj.bmjjournals.com/cgi/content/full/315/7120/1450.

———. "The Effect of Weapons: Defining Superfluous Injury

and Unnecessary Suffering," www.ippnw.org/MGS/ V3.

Csikszentmihaly, Mihaly. *Flow: The Psychology of Optimal Experience*. New York: Harper & Row, 1990.

David-Neel, Alexandra. *Mystiques et Magiciens du Tibet*. Paris: Plon, 1929.

————. *Voyage d'une parisienne a Lhassa*. Paris: Plon, 1972.

Del Vasto, Lanza. *Le Pèlerinage aux Sources*. Paris: Folio, 1943.

————. *Technique de la Non-Violence*. Paris: Denoel, 1971.

De Troyes, Chretien. *Perceval ou le Roman du Graal*. Paris: Gallimard, 1974.

Duffey, Michael K. *Peacemaking Christians: The Future of Just Wars, Pacifism, and Nonviolent Resistance*. Kansas City: Sheed and Ward, 1995.

Erasmus, Desiderus. "The Praise of Folly" in *The Essential Erasmus*. New York: Mentor, 1964.

Friesen, Duane K., and Gerald W. Schlabach, eds. *At Peace and Unafraid*. Scottdale, Pa.: Herald Press, 2005.

Gibbon, Edward. *The Decline and Fall of the Roman Empire*. London: Everyman, 1974.

Gilgamesh, translated by Herbert Mason. New York: Mentor, 1970.

Giono, Jean. *Ecrits Pacifistes*. Paris: Gallimard, 1939.

Girard, Rene. *Des Choses Cachees Depuis la Fondation du Monde*. Paris: Livre du Poche, 1978.

————. *Violence and the Sacred*. London: Johns Hopkins, 1977.

Grimmelshausen. *Simplicius Simplicissimus*. New York: Library of Liberal Arts, 1965.

Hobbes, Thomas. *Leviathan*. New York: Library of Liberal Arts, 1958.

Howard, John. *The State of the Prisons*. London: Dent, 1927.

Kant, Immanuel. *The Analytic of the Beautiful*. Indianapolis:

Bobbs-Merrill, 1963.

———. *Perpetual Peace*, edited by Lewis White Beck. New York: Macmillan, 1957.

King, Martin Luther, Jr. *Why We Can't Wait*. New York: Mentor, 1963.

Kot, Stanislaw. *Socinianism in Poland*, translated by Earl Wilbur. Boston: Starr King, 1957.

Kozol, Jonathan. *The Shame of the Nation*. New York: Random House, 2006.

Kropotkin, Peter. *Kropotkin's Revolutionary Pamphlets*. New York: Dover, 1972.

Kübler-Ross, Elisabeth. *On Death and Dying*. New York: MacMillan, 1969.

Levi-Strauss, Claude. *Tristes Tropiques*. Paris: Plon, 1955.

Lewis, C. S. *The Weight of Glory and Other Addresses*. New York: Macmillan, 1980.

Marcuse, Herbert. *A Critique of Pure Tolerance*. New York: Beacon, 1965.

———. *One Dimensional Man*. New York: Beacon, 1964.

Merton, Thomas. *Faith and Violence*. Notre Dame, Ind.: University of Notre Dame Press, 1968.

———. *The Seven Storey Mountain*. New York: Harcourt, 1948.

Mill, John Stuart. *On Liberty*. London: Penguin, 1972.

Mo Tzu. *Basic Writings*, translated by Burton Watson. New York: Columbia University Press, 1963.

Pascal, Blaise. *Pensées*. Paris: Bookking International, 1970.

Schlabach, Theron, and Richard T. Hughes, eds. *Proclaim Peace: Christian Pacifism from Unexpected Quarters*. Chicago: University of Illinois Press, 1997.

Schweitzer, Albert. *The Quest of the Historical Jesus*. New York: Macmillan, 1961.

Sharp, Gene. *There Are Realistic Alternatives*. Boston: Albert Einstein Institution, 2003.

Spengler, Oswald. *The Decline of the West*. New York: Vintage, 2006.

Thesiger, Wilfred. *The Marsh Arabs*. London: Penguin, 1967.

Tolstoy, Leo. *War and Peace*, translated by Ann Dunnigan. New York: Signet, 1968.

Toynbee, Arnold. *A Study of History*. Oxford: Oxford University Press, 1961.

Voltaire. *Candide ou L'Optimisme*. Paris: Larousse, 1996.

Weil, Simone. "L'Iliade ou le Poeme de la Force," *Oeuvres*. Paris: Gallimard, 1999.

The Author

Thomas Trzyna is a professor of English at Seattle Pacific University. His academic interests have included the study of forgiveness and research on grieving in the ethnic-studies classroom. He has been active in founding a seminary and counseling school, administering colleges, and working as a college accrediting and development specialist. He formerly served as vice president for academic affairs, Mars Hill Graduate School, in Bothell, Washington. Currently he is developing a new university in Vietnam to create sustainable peace and economic progress through education. Trzyna was born in Evanston, Illinois, and lives with his family in Seattle, where he attends the University Friends Meeting.